D1602504

STUDIES IN INTERNATIONAL BUSINESS

Also by Peter Buckley

THE HANDBOOK OF INTERNATIONAL TRADE
  (*editor with Michael Z. Brooke*)

NORTH–SOUTH DIRECT INVESTMENT IN THE EUROPEAN
  COMMUNITIES (*with Patrick Artisien*)

THE ECONOMIC THEORY OF THE MULTINATIONAL
  ENTERPRISE (*with Mark Casson*)

THE INDUSTRIAL RELATIONS PRACTICES OF FOREIGN-
  OWNED FIRMS IN BRITAIN (*with Peter Enderwick*)

EUROPEAN DIRECT INVESTMENT IN THE USA BEFORE
  WORLD WAR 1 (*with Brian R. Roberts*)

FOREIGN DIRECT INVESTMENT BY SMALLER UK FIRMS
  (*with Gerald D. Newbould and Jane C. Thurwell*)

THE FUTURE OF THE MULTINATIONAL ENTERPRISE
  (*with Mark Casson*)

THE MULTINATIONAL ENTERPRISE: Theory and Applications

MULTINATIONAL ENTERPRISES IN LESS DEVELOPED
  COUNTRIES (*editor with Jeremy Clegg*)

DIRECT INVESTMENT IN THE UNITED KINGDOM BY
  SMALLER EUROPEAN FIRMS (*with Zdenka Berkova and
Gerald D. Newbould*)

STUDIES IN INTERNATIONAL BUSINESS

Peter J. Buckley
Professor of Managerial Economics
University of Bradford Management Centre

Foreword by
Raymond Vernon

St. Martin's Press

First published in Great Britain 1992 by
THE MACMILLAN PRESS LTD
Houndmills, Basingstoke, Hampshire RG21 2XS
and London
Companies and representatives
throughout the world

A catalogue record for this book is available
from the British Library

ISBN 0–333–54610–5

Printed in Great Britain by
Billing and Sons Ltd, Worcester

First published in the United States of America 1992 by
Scholarly and Reference Division,
ST. MARTIN'S PRESS, INC.,
175 Fifth Avenue,
New York, N.Y. 10010

ISBN 0–312–07601–0

Library of Congress Cataloging-in-Publication Data
Buckley, Peter J., 1949–
Studies in international business / Peter J. Buckley ; foreword by
Raymond Vernon.
p. cm.
Includes index.
ISBN 0–312–07601–0
1. International business enterprises.   I. Title.
HD2755.5.B843   1992
338.8'8—dc20   91–44083
                                                          CIP

For Thomas Robert

Contents

Foreword

At long last, the world is awakening to the fact that the dazzling advances of the past few decades in the means of international transportation and communication are producing equally profound changes in the way in which enterprises conduct their business. The enterprises of the 1990s routinely span distances with an ease that could not have been comtemplated two or three decades ago, searching for opportunities and threats in distant places.

Have the academics who profess to analyze the behavior of the world's enterprises managed to keep up with this breathtaking rate of change? The answer is a reluctant "not quite." Here and there one finds a revealing case study. Even more rarely, one encounters a brilliant effort at synthesis. But the pace of change is so swift as to defy most efforts to provide an altogether satisfying explanation of the evolving behavior of multinational enterprises.

The hallmark of Peter J. Buckley's work is that he has never ceased to try. At any moment, his work sits on the research frontier, raising issues and proposing hypotheses that will influence the direction of the research to follow.

That propensity sometimes carries Buckley into areas that are a little daunting for those who are expected to follow. Among academics, the study of multinational enterprises naturally enough tends to follow the structure of the academic disciplines. Economists study the behavior of such enterprises, as a rule, in terms with which economists are comfortable, that is, as a problem in the economic theory of the firm. Political scientists dissect their behavior as an aspect of international relations. Sociologists tackle the effort at understanding as a problem in group behavior. Savants in business schools, observing the enterprise in closer focus, tend to break down its functions into the usual familiar categories: finance, marketing, production, organizational structure, governmental relations, and so on. Without losing sight of these elements in the puzzle, Buckley resolutely resists these one-dimensional views of the elephant, searching for the formulation that will preserve a sense of its many dimensions. So politics, history, and culture take a place alongside the motivations that Adam Smith and Max Weber so aptly described.

The inexorable shrinkage of space that has characterized these past few decades shows no signs of diminishing, bringing with it a succession of consequences for which none of us is fully prepared. Superficially, the various national economies appear to be converging in their institutional forms and in their ways of doing business. But the increased intimacy among economies also seems to highlight the differences that remain, increasing the economic, political, and social importance of those remaining differences. Buckley's work helps to diminish the ignorance with which scholars, politicians, and businessmen observe the business behavior of those from other cultures. That increased understanding, one can hope, will also diminish the inescapable tensions that the increased intimacy is bound to generate.

Raymond Vernon

Acknowledgements

This book contains nine articles in the area of international business. Four of the articles are co-authored and I would like to thank my co-authors (Mark Casson, Patrick Artisien, Hafiz Mirza and John Sparkes) for their help. I have worked closely with each of them over a long period and appreciate their assistance, which is wider than simple research cooperation. I would also like to thank Ray Vernon for writing the foreword and his help and encouragement.

I am grateful for the permission of the copyright holders to reprint those articles which have appeared elsewhere. Chapters 1 and 6 appeared in *Journal of International Business Studies*, Volume 21, no. 4, 1990, and Volume 16, no. 1, 1985. Chapter 2 appeared in *Management International Review*, Special Issue 1991. Chapter 3 was first published in *Multinational Enterprises in Less Developed Countries*, edited by Peter J. Buckley and Jeremy Clegg and published by Macmillan, London, in 1991. Chapter 5 is taken from *Journal of Economic Issues* Vol. XXIII, no. 3, 1989, and Chapter 7 from *Japan Forum* Volume II, no. 2, 1990. Chapter 8 first appeared in *Japanese and European Management: Their International Adaptability* edited by Kazuo Shibagaki, Malcolm Trevor and Tetsuo Abo, published by University of Tokyo Press, Tokyo 1989. Chapter 6 is formerly unpublished. Individual acknowledgements are given in each Chapter but I would, in addition, like to record my thanks to the editors of the volumes concerned.

It is also appropriate to thank the institutions where this work has been nurtured. My primary debt is to the University of Bradford Management Centre, which under its past and current directors, Chris Higgins and David Weir, has been an excellent base from which to produce research. I would also like to thank other institutions which have weathered my incursions as Visiting Professor – the Department of Economics, University of Reading under the Chairmanship of Mark Casson and Oslo Business School (Handelshoyschole) where thanks are due to Stig Herbern and Pervez Ghauri. My debts for secretarial assistance go once again to Mrs Sylvia Ashdown and Mrs Chris Barkby.

Peter J. Buckley

Notes on the Other Contributors

Patrick Artisien is Lecturer in International Business and Economics, Cardiff Business School, University of Wales.

Mark Casson is Professor of Economics, University of Reading.

Hafiz Mirza is Senior Lecturer in International Business, University of Bradford Management Centre.

John R. Sparkes is Professor of Business Economics, University of Bradford Management Centre.

Part I

Theory

1 Problems and Developments in the Core Theory of International Business*

Peter J. Buckley

ABSTRACT

The established theory of international business is not without problems. It is necessary to specify the key relationships between internalisation and market structure and between internalisation and competitive advantage more carefully. This chapter attempts to clarify the former relationship by reference to the work of Hymer and the latter by contrasting the nature of internalisation decisions with those building short-run competitive advantage. Avenues of development of the theory include the integration of non-traditional concepts and the reintegration of areas of research which have become divorced from core international business theory.

INTRODUCTION

It is now generally agreed that an established theory of the multinational enterprise exists. The synthesis is based on internalisation theory, the theory of location and competitive dynamics. An outline of this position together with the difficulties of empirical testing was given in an earlier article (Buckley 1988). The synthesis relies on fundamental concepts derived from Coase (1937), Kaldor (1934), modern industrial organisation theory, international trade theory and theories of monopoly and monopolistic

---

* I am grateful for the comments of three anonymous referees on a previous draft. These comments have improved the paper in various directions which are not individually noted.

competition (notably the inheritors of the tradition begun by Hymer 1976). However, a number of problems remain in this emerging 'core theory'. This paper attempts to elucidate these problems and to suggest avenues of development.

Two issues of current importance in core internalisation theory are examined – the relationship between internalisation decisions and market structure and between internalisation and competitive advantage. These issues look to be technicalities. In fact, they illustrate some of the key problems that new approaches must confront.

PROBLEMS IN CORE THEORY

1. **The relationship between internalisation decisions and market structure**

It has become fashionable for analysts to draw a distinction between theories based on internalisation (as exemplified by Buckley and Casson (1976, 1985)) and those based on market power (exemplified by Hymer 1976). An example of this line of argument is Cantwell (1988). The two are not mutually exclusive, or competing, theories but need to be combined to give a full and rich explanation of the growth of multinational firms. Such an explanation becomes complicated because of the interaction between internalisation decisions and market outcomes.

The source of clues on ways to integrate these approaches is a surprising one – Hymer himself. In a recently rediscovered paper originally written in French (Hymer 1968; Casson 1989), Hymer provides a heuristic explanation of the interaction of the internalisation of markets and market structure. Two sets of processes are at work. (1) Internalisation decisions, with industry size fixed, determine the number of firms in the industry. (2) (i) Market structure governs the opportunities for horizontal expansion, so that highly concentrated industries encourage diversification and (ii) particular market structures result in imperfections that induce price distortions within multistage processes, thus providing incentives for forward or backward integration. These outcomes then feed back to a further round of internalisation decisions. Thus a dynamic process of interaction is described. In a static or slowly-evolving world this interaction is likely to converge on an equilibrium. A crude form of this model is shown as Figure 1.1. This framework is capable of extension and of encompassing many current theoretical developments. For example, the choice of diversification into new product areas at home or internationalisation in the same product area has been

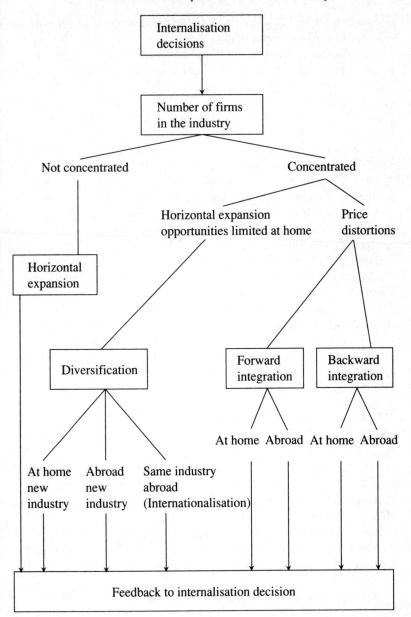

FIGURE 1.1   The interaction between internalisation decisions and market structure (after Hymer [1968])

discussed by Wolf (1977). There are also possibilities of an approach to
business strategy more grounded in theory.

The political economy implications of the difference in approach between internalisation-based theories and those which emphasise market
power should be not ignored. In work which post-dates his 1968 paper
Hymer integrated the 'Law of Increasing Firm Size' with 'The Law of
Uneven Development' to provide a powerful critique of the multinational
enterprise as an institution (Hymer 1970, 1971). Paradoxically, the other
major contributor to the Hymer–Kindleberger approach emphasised the
role of multinationals in improving efficiency by increasing global competition, breaking up domestic monopolies and surmounting government-
imposed barriers to freer competition (Kindleberger 1969).

A synthesis of these views on the welfare impact of multinationals
recognises both welfare gains and welfare losses from the establishment
and growth of multinational enterprises. Welfare gains arise when the
replacement of an imperfect external market results in the superior allocation of resources in the internal market and where a new market is created
where none existed before (internalisation of an externality). Welfare losses
arise where multinationals maximise monopoly profits by restricting the
output of goods and services and where vertical integration is used as a
barrier to entry. Further, multinationals may reduce social efficiency because they provide a more suitable mechanism for exploiting a collusive
agreement than does a cartel. By internalising a collusive agreement, multinationals make the enforcement of collusion more effective (Casson 1985;
Buckley 1989a).

The dynamic elements in welfare effects are also important. An internal
market allows greater inter-plant integration (Scherer *et al.* 1975) and cross-
functional integration within the firm (e.g. between production, marketing
and R & D) and in the long run this will stimulate both the undertaking of
R & D and its effective implementation in production and marketing.
Consequently, dynamic welfare improvement is likely to result from more
effective developments in technology.

It is clear that the welfare implications of the operations of multinationals
require careful analysis and greater attention to empirical detail. It is also
arguable that political and social variables require more attention.

2. Internalisation and competitive advantage

In the internalisation approach the firm is seen as an internalised bundle of
resources which can be allocated (i) between product groups (changes in
which are identified as conglomerate diversification) and (ii) between

national markets (expansion in this direction is multinational diversification). The growth of the firm *relative to markets* is determined by its internalisation decisions. The firm grows by replacing or creating neighbouring markets according to the (positive) balance between the benefits of internalisation versus the costs in each instance. The growth of the firm, in this analysis, is determined by the net benefits of internal control relative to the extra cost of using imperfect external markets in intermediate products and services (Buckley and Casson 1976, 1985; Buckley 1983; Casson 1987; Buckley 1988).

However, in the models of competitive advantage deriving from the competitive strategy approach (Porter 1980, 1985, 1986), competitive advantage is defined as the advantage of one firm *relative to another firm*. Thus a firm can have a relative cost advantage, deriving for example from economies of scale, an absolute cost advantage deriving from control of key inputs, superior product technology or cheaper physical distribution, and product differentiation advantages arising from superior products or more effective marketing. The concept of competitive advantage as used by Porter is directly analogous to Dunning's firm-specific advantage (Dunning 1981).

Unfortunately there has often been a confusion in the literature between the concepts of internalisation and competitive advantage. The nature of these concepts is, in fact, very different both from an analytical point of view and from a strategic viewpoint. In contrast to the long-run nature of internalisation benefits, it is a feature of competitive advantages that they must be defined over a given fixed time period, for it is possible for competing firms to catch up by rearranging their resources to mimic or overtake the 'leader' (defined as the firm with the greatest net competitive advantages). It is implicit, and often explicit, in models of competitive advantage that such advantages exist in imperfectly competitive markets, although the nature of the imperfection is not always spelled out. When these imperfections are made explicit, it is possible to begin to see the interaction between internalisation and competitive advantages. Much play is made of superior technology possessed by leading firms in the competitive advantages model. In fact this result requires additional assumptions on the nature of diffusion of technical know how (Buckley 1983). The firm as a device for slowing the rate of diffusion of innovation (Johnson 1970) or as an 'appropriator' of technological rent (Magee 1977a, 1977b) is a key strand in this element of competitive advantage. The time span of such a technological lead will be limited (by the capability of followers to copy the technology). However, there may be long-run advantages of internalising the R & D function with the production function to facilitate the smooth transition of research into commercialised production. There are costs too; firms can be locked into obsolescent technology through a captive R & D unit. Care should be taken in distinguishing the long-run benefits and costs of internalised R & D units from competitive advantages given in the short run by a technological lead.

Similar arguments apply to the marketing function. There are advantages given by integrating production and marketing – and costs too. However, these vertical integration agruments apply to management versus the market. The competitive advantage literature concerns the superiority of one firm's management over another. Competitive advantages are a measure of net wealth arising from past entrepreneurial activity and *at a point of time* are differentially available to individual firms. The key strategy issue is to derive maximum benefit from this net wealth by deploying it effectively. Hence the need to identify strengths and weaknesses relative to competitors and potential competitors and to seek to minimise threats and take advantage of opportunities, in the language of business strategists.

In this shorter run, strategic context, internalisation can be a weapon. Internalising the market in key inputs (including technology) can represent a significant barrier to entry to the industry. The ability to use discriminatory pricing in an internal market allows a firm to cross-subsidise highly competitive markets where there is a fear of entry. Elimination of bilateral bargaining may further strengthen a firm relative to others faced with bargaining instability. Further, internalisation of markets across international frontiers allows the reduction of the firm's overall tax bill relative to firms who trade at arm's length. Consequently, internalisation decisions can be a strategic weapon versus other firms in certain contexts. It is undeniable that certain managements will see internalisation opportunities faster than others and may be more skilled at the evaluation of such opportunities. This will create differentials in the relative scope of firms with cost penalties for those with non-optimal scope (at a given point of time).

AVENUES OF DEVELOPMENT

1. **The integration of non-traditional concepts**

International business and multinational enterprises do not exist in a vacuum. They are profoundly affected not only by economic changes but also by social and political change. Consequently the core theory of international business must expand beyond the narrow economistic approach to encompass social and political effects. Such an integration, however desirable (Casson

1988a; Dunning 1989; Buckley 1989a), is not straightforward. It is not possible simply to 'bolt on' non-traditional or unorthodox concepts from political science, sociology or geography and social anthropology (Buckley and Casson 1989; Casson 1988b). The integration of such concepts will perforce proceed piecemeal. It is therefore essential to examine the theory for linking points with such concepts in the hope of building bridges which will bear the weight which they must carry.

One such bridge is the concept of entrepreneurship. This crucial aspect of decision-making has long played a role in growth and development theory (Schumpeter 1934). It is also at the heart of much business strategy theorising. The conceptualisation of entrepreneurial activity is no easy task (Casson 1982, 1988b) and its integration with analyses of business strategy is a problem which has not yet been tackled successfully.

The concept of internalisation is itself a bridge to other areas. An example of this is linkages with writings on organisation theory, notably the resource dependence approach. The classic reference is Pfeffer and Salancik (1978). Such a link could reinforce the hypotheses on the directional dynamics underlying the growth of firms (Buckley 1983).

2. Reintegration of the subject

The avenue of development outlined above may lead to a degree of diffuseness or fragmentation in a core theory which has previously had the quality of coherence or 'tightness'. The widening of concepts is essential to encompass the changing realities of the world economy. However, in so doing international business theory may well be able to capture areas that have to some degree disengaged from the core theory. An example of this potential recapture is the reinvigorated field of international trade theory. Trade theory has moved away from its strict neoclassical straitjacket to becoming policy-orientated and closely related to business strategy. The new 'strategic trade theory' takes on board the complications brought about by imperfect markets. It is not necessary to accept the policy conclusions that emerge to acknowledge the importance of this development. In the medium term, developments in strategic trade theory make full integration with the economic theory of the multinational enterprise much easier. (For reviews see Rugman 1986; Buckley 1989a; see also Ethier 1986; Helpman and Krugman 1985).

The possibilities of reintegration of strategic trade theory into the core theory of international business are symptoms of a wider phenomenon. Concepts from international business are beginning to spill over to neighbouring disciplines and to achieve linkages that pull in related concepts.

This is happening in the area of economics, broadly defined. However, it is not the standard marginalist, neoclassical elements of economics that are proving most useful but the somewhat unorthodox classical, Austrian and mercantilist strands of economic thought which are most relevant. Again, let one example stand for evidence in each case. Classical growth theory, as expounded by Adam Smith (1776) and reinterpreted by Josef Schumpeter (1934) puts disequilibrium states and dynamic change as instituted by the entrepreneur at the centre of the stage. Austrian approaches to market processes and entrepreneurial foresight are central to the dynamics of business change and development. (Kirzner 1973, 1979; Mises 1963).

The statism exemplified by Friedrich List (1840) is being reinterpreted to provide a basic theory for the 'developmental state' literature which is felt to be an appropriate model for Japan (and possibly for Korea and other newly-industrialising economies). (Johnson 1982).

The common thread of these approaches is attention to dynamics and disequilibrium at the levels of the firm, markets and international competitors. This gives a surprisingly contemporary feel to the concepts.

CONCLUSION

The core theory of international business is a well-established basis on which future research can proceed. In common with any other theoretical approach, developments must steer a course between analysing reality and relative simplicity. This trade-off will vary with the task in hand and particularly with the problem that theory is attempting to tackle. Extension of the core theory is necessary in view of the impact of social and political changes which cannot be taken as residuals. This extension requires careful redefinition of the relationship between key explanatory variables so that new developments grow organically from the theory rather than being added in a piecemeal and arbitrary fashion.

References

Buckley, Peter J. 1983. 'New theories of international business: Some unresolved issues', in Mark Casson (ed.), *The Growth of International Business* (London: George Allen & Unwin).
Buckley, Peter J. 1988. 'The limits of explanation: Testing the internationalisation theory of the multinational enterprise', *Journal of International Business Studies*, Summer, 2: 181–93.

Buckley, Peter J. 1989a. 'The frontiers of international business research', University of Bradford *mimeo*.

Buckley, Peter J. 1989b. 'On Japanese foreign direct investment', in Peter J. Buckley, *The Multinational Enterprise: theory and application* (London: Macmillan).

Buckley, Peter J. and Mark Casson. 1976. *The Future of the Multinational Enterprise* (London: Macmillan).

Buckley, Peter J. and Mark Casson. 1985. *The Economic Analysis of the Multinational Enterprise: Selected Papers* (London: Macmillan).

Buckley, Peter J. and Mark Casson. 1989. 'Multinational enterprises in less developed countries: Cultural and economic interactions.' University of Reading Discussion Papers in International Investment and Business Studies, No. 126, January (forthcoming in Buckley and Clegg, 1990, *Multinational Enterprises in Less Developed Countries* (London: Macmillan).

Cantwell, John A. 1988. 'Theories of international production', University of Reading Discussion Papers in International Investment and Business Studies, No. 122, September.

Casson, Mark. 1982. *The Entrepreneur: An economic theory* (Oxford: Martin Robertson).

Casson, Mark. 1985. 'Multinational monopolies and international cartels', in Peter J. Buckley and Mark Casson, *The Economic Theory of the Multinational Enterprise* (London: Macmillan).

Casson, Mark. 1987. *The Firm and the Market* (Oxford: Basil Blackwell).

Casson, Mark. 1988a. 'The theory of international business as a unified social science', University of Reading discussion papers in international investment and business studies, No. 123, November.

Casson, Mark. 1988b. 'Entrepreneurial culture as a competitive advantage', University of Reading Discussion Papers in International Investment and Business Studies, No. 124, November.

Casson, Mark. 1989. Introduction to 'The large multinational "corporation": An analysis of some motives for the international integration of business' by Stephen H. Hymer. University of Reading *mimeo*.

Coase, Ronald H. 1937. 'The nature of the firm', *Economica* (New Series) 4: 386–405.

Dunning, John H. 1981. *International Production and the Multinational Enterprise* (London: George Allen & Unwin).

Dunning, John H. 1989. 'The study of international business: A plea for a more interdisciplinary approach', University of Reading Discussion Papers in International Investment and Business Studies, No. 127, February.

Ethier, Wilfred J. 1986. 'The multinational firm', *Quarterly Journal of Economics*, November, 4: 805–83.

Helpman, Elhanan and Paul Krugman. 1985. *Market Structure and Foreign Trade* (Cambridge, Mass.: MIT Press).

Hymer, Stephen H. 1968. 'The large multinational "corporation". An analysis of some motives for the international integration of business', *Revue Economique*, 19, 6: 949–73. Translated by Nathalie Vacherot, Introduction by Mark Casson 1989. University of Reading, *mimeo*.

Hymer, Stephen H. 1970. 'The efficiency (contradictions) of the multinational corporation'. *Papers and Proceedings of the American Economic Association*, May.

Hymer, Stephen H. 1971. 'The multinational corporation and the law of uneven development', in J. N. Bhagwati (ed.), *Economics and World Order* (New York: World Law Fund).

Hymer, Stephen H. 1976. *The International Operations of National Firms* (Cambridge, Mass.: MIT Press).

Johnson, Chalmers. 1982. *MITI and the Japanese Miracle: The growth of industrial policy 1925–1975* (Stanford: Stanford University Press).

Johnson, Henry G. 1970. 'The efficiency and welfare implications of the international corporation', in C. P. Kindelberger (ed.), *The International Corporation* (Cambridge, Mass.: MIT Press).

Kaldor, N. 1934. 'The equilibrium of the firm', *Economic Journal*, March.

Kindleberger, C. P. 1969. *American Business Abroad* (New Haven: Yale University Press).

Kirzner, Israel M. 1973. *Competition and Entrepreneurship* (Chicago: University of Chicago Press).

Kirzner, Israel M. 1979. *Perception, Opportunity and Profit* (Chicago: University of Chicago Press).

List, Friedrich. 1840. *Das nationale system der politischen oekonomie* (Stuttgart, Tubingen). Translated as *The National System of Political Economy*.

Magee, Stephen P. 1977a. 'Multinational corporations, industry technology cycle and development', *Journal of World Trade Law*: 297–321.

Magee, Stephen P. 1977b. 'Information and the multinational corporation: An appropriability theory of direct foreign investment', in J. N. Baghwati (ed.), *The New International Economic Order* (Cambridge, Mass.: MIT Press).

Mises, Ludwig Von. 1963. *Human Action: A treatise on economics* (2nd edition) (New Haven: Yale University Press).

Pfeffer, Jeffrey and Gerald Salancik. 1978. *The External Control of Organisations: A resource dependence perspective* (New York: Harper and Row).

Porter, Michael E. 1980. *Competitive Strategy: Techniques for analysing industries and competitors* (New York: Free Press).

Porter, Michael E. 1985. *Competitive Advantage: Creating and sustaining superior performance* (New York: Free Press).

Porter, Michael E. (ed.). 1986. *Competition in Global Industries* (Boston: Harvard University Press).

Rugman, Alan M. 1986. 'New theories of the multinational enterprise: An assessment of internalisation theory' *Bulletin of Economic Research*, 2: 101–18.

Scherer, F. M. et al. (1975). *The Economics of Multi-plant Operation – An international comparisons study* (Cambridge Mass.: Harvard University Press).

Schumpeter, J. A. (1934). *The Theory of Economic Development* (Cambridge, Mass: Harvard University Press).

Smith, Adam. 1776. *An Inquiry into the Nature and Causes of the Wealth of Nations*, ed. R. H. Campbell, A. S. Skinner and W. B. Todd, (Oxford: Clarendon Press, 1976).

Wolf, Bernard M. 1977. 'Industrial diversification and internationalisation: Some empirical evidence'. *Journal of Industrial Economics*, December, 2: 177–91.

2 The Frontiers of International Business Research[*]

Peter J. Buckley

ABSTRACT

This chapter reviews recent key developments in international business research. It develops from a core framework based on the internalisation and location decisions of firms to the wider concepts necessary to encompass the crucial variables suggested by a variety of analysts. Developments towards interdisciplinarity are noted. These are necessary to encompass variables such as culture and cooperation between firms which are often treated as residuals. The challenge and pitfalls of comparative research are examined as is the desire to go deeper into questions of competitiveness and development. The incorporation of new concepts must not detract from rigour. The appearance of diffuseness will be supplanted by a research framework richer and eventually more coherent than those currently available.

THE FRONTIERS OF INTERNATIONAL BUSINESS RESEARCH

An earlier article (Buckley 1988) attempted to give a view of the current position of international business research. This article is an attempt to go beyond 'The limits of explanation' to identify key research questions which have not been fully confronted. In order to do this, it is necessary to have a firm theoretical base, otherwise the building will be on unsafe ground, with results graphically described in Matthew 7.[1] The theoretical base used is that based on internalisation theory and location costs as described in Buckley (1988). This approach is a good means of organising, explaining

[*] I would like to thank Professor Mark Casson (University of Reading) for comments on an earlier draft.

13

and predicting the pattern of multinational enterprise and its growth. The argument of this paper is that the basic approach needs to be widened and deepened in order to take full cognizance of differences among and between firms and countries.

Future developments in international business

There appear to be a number of exciting frontier areas of international business research. From the most general to the most specific, they can be listed as follows.

1.   Interdisciplinary approaches to international business.
2.   Comparative (cross-national) studies, e.g. of industrial policy.
3.   Developments in international trade theory, encompassing foreign direct investment and strategic moves by firms and countries.
4.   Studies of international competitiveness.
5.   Renewed interest in the role of the multinational enterprise in less developed countries.
6.   The analysis of joint ventures, alliances and cooperative forms of business activities.
7.   Studies of service industries.

The article examines each of these areas with a view to their likely potential yield in theoretical developments. In assessing theory we must not forget empirical evidence. It is clear that the entry of Japan as a first-rate world economic power has given a major stimulus to international business research, as has the contrast between the growth of the Newly Industrialising Countries (NICs) and the stagnation and indeed decline of several of the least developed countries of the world. New data, on multinationals from the less developed countries[2] and on foreign direct investment from and to important but neglected countries (like Italy) have broadened perspectives and widened the research outlook beyond its traditional base. 'New' management practices such as total quality management (TQM), just-in-time inventory control and performance budgeting have generated new information and engendered new possibilities. All of this is grist to the mill of the international business researcher. But it is essential to have a clear theoretical understanding: otherwise, naive projections will result.

   This analysis takes place from a positive point of view on international business research. The major strength of international business research is that it tackles the 'big questions' head on. It is encouraging that other branches of the social sciences also see the need to tackle wider themes.

KEY DEVELOPMENTS IN INTERNATIONAL BUSINESS
RESEARCH

1. Interdisciplinary approaches to international business

The development of the academic study of international business has come
from the core disciplines: finance, marketing, economics, etc. Specialisms
such as international finance have developed by extension of concepts to
the international sphere. As in the case of the longest-established such area
– international economics – international study has enlivened the subject
and has fed back concepts and new empirical work into the discipline.
However, there has been little cross-fertilisation across (international) disciplines. Developments have been 'vertical' rather than 'horizontal'.

However, there are signs that this state of affairs is changing. Recently,
a number of articles have appeared advocating a greater degree of
interdisciplinarity (or transdisciplinarity) in the approach to international
business. Toyne (1989) advocates an approach based on a view of international exchange as a process, thus incorporating dynamic elements.
Dunning (1989) has an ingenious and appealing line of argument which
sees scholars (and disciplines) as complementary assets, needing to be
combined in optimum proportions for maximum efficiency. Casson (1988a)
takes this further by considering international business as a test case for a
unified social science approach. This parallels his work on entrepreneurship
(1988b) which acknowledges that a single-discipline approach to the key
dynamic force of entrepreneurship is likely to be found wanting.

Researchers in international business will be familiar with the key difficulty
in this area – the argument that 'the cobbler should stick to his last' and
warnings not to dabble in other experts' areas. This is a challenge which
must be confronted. It can be met by the individual scholar going back to
the drawing board (or desk) and learning anew. Or it can be met by the
building of interdisciplinary teams and confronting the language, culture
and other boundaries which separate disciplines. The moulding of core
concepts across disciplines is extremely difficult. However, the information
in international business lends itself to interdisciplinary interpretation –
how many times do economists relegate 'culture' to a residual, unmeasurable
therefore unimportant status – in their key models? Practising what is
preached is difficult, however. A modest start has been made by Buckley
and Casson (1989) in combining economics, geography and social anthropology focused on the issue of multinational enterprises in less developed
countries. A link can be made for instance between culture and the technical
concept of transaction costs by the observation that the cohesion of

particular societies may enable the reduction of transaction costs because of high levels of trust between members of the society, which reduces the necessity for legal recourse or guarantees. Boddewyn (1988) applies internalisation theory to markets in political influence and information. This extension works extremely well, because of the care with which the concepts are applied and it appears to provide an illuminating insight into an area previously considered conceptually intractable.

There is a strong case in interdisciplinary work for going back in time beyond the fragmentation of the business disciplines to work which predates a separate area of business studies. Casson goes back to Babbage (1832), Schumpeter (1934) and Frank Knight (1935) as well as, of course, Adam Smith (1776). The internalisation framework itself dates from that key period in micro-economic formulations, the 1930s (Coase 1937); see also Kaldor (1934).

In attempting to synthesise disparate key concepts, Buckley (1988) traces the impact of (1) social and political changes, (2) changes in technology and technique and (3) changes in tastes/demand on two instrumental variables – changes in relative cost conditions and changes in the international division of labour. Buckley and Casson (1989) go even further back to search out the factors which underlie competitive advantage – into the development of an entrepreneurial culture and geographical elements which confer entrepôt potential as an initial locational advantage. This locational advantage interacts with entrepreneurial process (e.g. the development of systems thinking) into virtuous circles of development or into areas of constraints arising from blocked expansion paths spatially or the breakdown of the cultural dynamic. This searching backwards both in time and in deeper sources of the rather superficially-used concept of 'competitive advantage' are likely to give the impression of fragmentation of the discipline or of excessive attention to *minutiae*, in the short run. In the long run, however, a much richer vein of theorising will result. A by-product of this avenue is likely to be the downgrading of Anglo-Saxon conceptual domination because of the rediscovery of (particularly) Continental European antecedents. It is likely that this rediscovery will include such social scientists as Weber and Durkheim as well as the more obvious sources such as Schumpeter (1934).

The tradition represented by Weber and Durkheim is very much interdisciplinary and comparative. Weber's work on economic history (1923), social and economic organisation (1947), and the inter-relationships of religion and economic development (1930; 1965) as well as general insights into social science methodology (1949) make him an exemplary source for insights into long-run international development issues. Durkheim's work at the interface of sociology and economics (notably on the division of labour in society (1964)) is also paralleled by studies with profound insights into the impact of culture, and particularly religious culture, on society (1915).

2. Comparative studies in international business

Nowhere is the impact of the entry of Japan as a first-rate economic power as obvious as in the renewed interest in comparative studies. The comparative study of industrial policy is a key development here. 'Comparative management' as a subject in its own right has a long history and has been instructive in the attention it has drawn to the conceptual and empirical pitfalls in comparative work.

Much of the difficulty and excitement of comparative research lies in the area of methodology. (See Lonner and Berry 1986). An illustration of the difficulties and frustrations of comparative analysis was recently given by Adler, Campbell and Laurent (1989). The comparative perspective is particularly challenging because, as Etzioni and DuBow [(1970) p. viii] point out 'the comparative perspective is more than a scientific technique – it provides a basic intellectual outlook'. There can be few of us who do not believe that we have something to learn from other cultures and societies, but the issues of how real differences are to be identified and how they relate to other elements in society are of crucial analytical importance. A current illustration of this is the controversy over the transferability or otherwise of Japanese management practices. Are these practices rooted in unique Japanese cultural traits? Or can they be extracted, transferred and transplanted on a piecemeal basis? Such controversies are not new. In 1952 Arnold Toynbee opined that fragments of a culture, such as its technological advances, were much more likely to have an impact on another culture than an attempt to introduce a way of life *en bloc* (Toynbee 1953). This piecemeal absorption, he goes on to note, may have profound long-term effects, pulling in related elements from the exported culture. How often have we observed developing countries' desire to obtain advanced technology without the associated cultural dominance? Lest this be thought to be far removed from international business practice, note the increase in 'new forms' of non-equity technology deals under pressure from this demand.

Difficulties of conceptualisation of the units of comparison and cross-cultural verification (Etzioni and DuBow 1970, Introduction) are compounded when one of the major actors, the multinational enterprise, is actually itself a transnational entity.

The basic problem in comparative research arises from the monumental nature of the task. The great strength of comparative research is that it provides a carefully specified 'counterfactual' – the situation existing in the country with which comparisons are being drawn. However, difficulties arise from abstracting from the investigator's own cultural bias, which is likely to impinge on objectivity (Campbell 1970). The method of comparative research is very precise. Indeed it is analytically more rigorous than single-country studies, as it provides measurable counterfactuals. However, the difficulty of carrying it out arises from the large amount of information necessary. Because of this a focus on 'the local, the concrete, the specific' (Rokkan 1970) is more likely to lead to immediate, short-term results than the careful design of comparative work. A further obvious, but important difficulty exists. This is language difference in comparative research. Even the most expert translations and retranslations can produce differences of meaning (Phillips 1970; Briskin 1986). The underlying difficulty arises in the nuances of meaning as expressed through language. Cultural biases in language are not easy to exclude.

The large amount of information necessary has a further analytical drawback. In amassing the information it is difficult to avoid secondary sources – primary data being so expensive and time-consuming to collect. This means that the analyst is often constrained to take the analysis implicit or explicit in the secondary source as well as the raw information. Comparative research thus often has to rely on an assembly of different and disparate data (and experts), which can cause problems.

3. Developments in international trade theory

If the theory of international trade could ever be ignored by international business specialists, the moment has passed. Trade theory, from being an exercise in high theory, has suddenly become an area with an intense pragmatic policy orientation. A stronger political dimension has been introduced – largely because of debates on the Japanese threat to other advanced nations. This move towards the 'new mercantilism' has exposed some of the unrealistic assumptions of pure theory to the invigorating breath of pragmatism. The role of technological elements in trade theory has never been far below the surface and a new thread of technological competition has been woven into the emerging framework. The renewed interest in international trade theory comes about because of the attempts of trade theorists to incorporate foreign investment and the multinational enterprise into simple general equilibrium models of the world economy. This is combined with the increased interest in 'strategic trade policy' which reopens the debate on restrictions of trade for national welfare purposes. Developments in trade theory thus heighten the debate on the welfare implications of multinationals.

In 1983 Krugman said, 'The theoretical models of trade, factor move-ments and protection, which are the essence of standard trade theory, have no role for direct foreign investment . . .. The reason for this peripheral position is not hard to find. At the root of conventional models in interna-tional trade is the assumption of perfect competition; but any theory of the multinational firm must come to grips with imperfect competition' (Krugman 1983, p. 57). In fact a number of attempts had been made to integrate the standard Hecksher–Ohlin theory of trade with international investment, amongst them Casson (1979), and Markusen (1981).

The essential difficulties arise from the necessity to incorporate the internalisation decision in response to market imperfections. Krugman (1983) went on to introduce two models, one covering product differentiation, the other a vertical integration model. Developments since this time have been a vindication of this line of analysis. Several crucial problems, however, remain to be solved.

The debate takes place in the traditional Hecksher–Ohlin, two-factor, two-country, two-goods model. However, the key developments concern the introduction of specialised inputs linked to proprietary technology and analogous to public goods within the firm (antecedents are Coase 1937; Caves 1971; and Buckley and Casson 1976). In many cases (Helpman 1984 Helpman and Krugman, 1985; Markusen 1984) the internalisation decision is taken for granted. (For a similar opinion see Rugman 1986). However Ethier (1986) has attempted to model internalisation as a response to moni-toring quality, or rather controlling the information necessary to monitor quality. Arm's length intermediate trade can be distinguished from internal-ised intermediate trade, and thus the incentive to form multinationals by internalising intermediate trade is given where this leads to a more efficient equilibrium.

A major difficulty with models other than that of Ethier is that they concern only the location decision, being analyses of the choice between exporting and foreign investment rather than incorporating the choice between equity and non-equity foreign involvement.

However, a recent article by Horstmann and Markusen (1989) attempts to encompass the welfare effects of direct foreign investment in a simple general equilibrium model. International competitive advantages are mod-elled as knowledge-based, firm specific assets with public good character-istics. Gains to the host country occur where competition drives down average costs and where the host country is too small to support a domestic firm. Costs occur where the foreign investor drives out a profitable domestic rival. The model shows welfare gains to the source country, admittedly under rather restrictive assumptions. This approach promises future gains in welfare analysis.

A more radical approach to the analysis of trade in intermediate goods is given by Casson (1985) in a paper which extends and formalises the work of Dunning and others and also gives the theory of location a radical twist. First, Casson suggests that factor substitution has a very limited role in the location of production. The effect of this proposition is that the Ricardian theory of comparative labour costs assumes great significance. If capital is mobile, then the only significant margin is that at which labour is allocated between industries. As this margin differs at different locations, it will be a prime determinant of the pattern of international production.

Second, Casson argues that technical progress results in reductions in transport costs, greater economies of scale and promotion of the division of labour rather than factor-saving advances in production. In particular, the promotion of the division of labour has profound implications for the location of the activities of multinational firms. The subdivision of a productive activity creates a market for an intermediate product linking the first activity to the second. The division of labour can, as Casson notes, create a pyramid of activities in which both horizontal and vertical specialisation occurs – the activities at the 'bottom' produce components which are then combined in assembly processes higher in the pyramidal structure. When the intermediate products are tradeable, it becomes possible to separate spatially the activities and to replace one plant by two different ones, on which different location pressures now operate. The resulting increased specialisation enables cost reductions in economies of scale, lower input costs and transport costs.

Third, Casson suggests that proprietary technology, where access to knowledge is restricted, is an important barrier to entry, which encourages monopoly or oligopoly in the supply of new products. It is often advantageous for the monopolist to integrate backwards to control supplies of inputs or components embodied in the final product. This leads to the control of international production of new products by vertically integrated monopolistic MNEs.

The interaction of policy and theory in international business and trade theory is shown by the increasing importance of theoretical and empirical work in international integration in the wake of the US–Canada Free Trade Agreement and the Single European Market Act. In both cases the reaction of multinational firms is crucial to the outcome of the integration measures. It is vital to predict the behaviour of multinational firms already present in the market, both those which are owned by a home country in the market and those owned by a nation outside the market. It is also necessary to predict the behaviour of multinationals from major home countries outside the area undergoing integration. Thus predictions of the welfare impact of integration depend, for instance, on the behaviour of US car firms with subsidiaries in Canada in one case and the behaviour of Japanese multinationals exporting to Europe in the other. Will US car firms rationalise their pan-North American operations on lines suggested by the literature (i.e. increase vertical integration but decrease horizontal integration)? Will Japanese exporters to Europe switch their foreign market servicing policy in favour of direct investment? Both the theory of the multinational enterprise and the theory of economic integration can speak to these issues, but not yet in a fully unified fashion.

4. International competitiveness

Work on international competitiveness is important because it reintroduces national-level or macro concerns to international business. Much of the theoretical and empirical advances in international business have been micro-orientated. Indeed, they have been at the level of the firm rather than the industry or any higher level of aggregation. Moves towards higher levels of aggregation promise much in the relatively underdeveloped field of international political economy.

Competitiveness is a concept which goes beyond the economist's traditional notion of efficiency. Efficiency can be described as the optimal allocation of resources to achieve desired ends. The additional element in competitiveness is the choice of the most appropriate ends. In other words competitiveness includes both efficiency (reaching goals at the least possible cost) *and* effectiveness (having the right goals). Thus the concept includes both means and ends (Buckley, Pass and Prescott 1988). Further, competitiveness must be judged relative to some other state of the world. The possibilities are (1) relative to the situation at a different historical point of time (2) relative to an existing comparator (paired groups of firms or foreign competitors for instance) and (3) relative to a well-defined counterfactual position. From this standpoint, the importance of comparative work is again to the fore.

Competitiveness is thus an elusive concept. Attempts to encompass it in single measures are fraught with danger and seemed doomed to failure (Buckley, Pass and Prescott 1988). However, the use of multiple measures can lead to diffuseness of concepts, inability to measure and internal trade-offs. It is also necessary to discuss the level at which the analysis is to take place – nation, industry, firm or product.

One useful approach seems to be to examine performance, potential and management process as parts of an interactive dynamic concept of competitiveness. Regarding each of these three as 'black boxes', the most

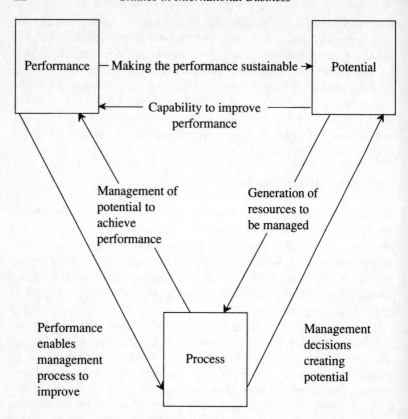

Source: Buckley, Pass and Prescott (1988), p. 178.

FIGURE 2.1   The interrelationship between measures of competitiveness

appropriate measures can be inserted into each (see Figure 2.1). In the British case at least, measures of performance (profitability and market share) seem to be almost universally accepted by all firms as appropriate measures of competitive performance. Measures of potential seem to be dependent on the industry studied and measures of management process are idiosyncratic to particular firms (Buckley, Pass and Prescott 1990).

5. The role of multinationals in less developed countries

Although the study of multinationals in less developed countries and the relationship between inward foreign direct investment and development have been subjects of study throughout the history of international business research, a considerable reappraisal is well underway. Policymakers in less developed countries now seem to be much more pragmatic in their approach to inward investment. This attitude is reflected in the altered stance of the United Nations Centre on Transnational Corporations (UNCTC), which has shifted away from its early position, highly critical of multinational firms and all their works.

The role of multinationals in LDCs is a major focus of the emerging interdisciplinary approach which looks set fair to begin resolving the problems which have beset this area of study in the past. The integration of concepts such as entrepreneurship and the impact of culture into mainstream analyses has gone far in this area of study as contributions to Buckley and Clegg (1990) show. The penetration of the host country not only by new technology but also by new management techniques, behaviour and attitudes can have a radical effect on social structure in the host country and may disrupt traditional patterns (e.g. the employment of women may conflict with local traditional norms). The link with social and political instability can thus be made explicit.

Together with new analytical approaches has come increased sophistication on the part of bargainers on the host-country side. This has led to a more realistic appraisal on both sides of the 'non zero-sum game' which inward direct investment represents. Both excessive expectations of the development benefits of multinational investment and the overplaying of dependency relationships have been deflated.

Conflicts still continue, however. The debate between export-led growth versus import substitution has been given a temporarily decisive shift by the growth performance of Japan and the NICs. However, there are few of the developing countries of Africa or the Indian subcontinent which can replicate the preconditions for growth present in Japan or the 'four little tigers'. A parallel trend towards the rolling-back of the state through privatisation again appears to present opportunities for multinationals and private host-country institutions to develop in previously controlled sectors by joint ventures and other cooperative modes. The attempt by many LDCs to develop downstream processing activities is reaching a crucial stage and the viability of these projects is currently subject to scrutiny.

The underlying issues of welfare and distribution remain. The market power of multinationals in small (even large) closed economies continues to create problems. Opening such economies to the winds of international competition may well destroy the domestically-owned indigenous sector. The introduction of more capital-intensive techniques by multinationals remains a subject of controversy both analytically and empirically. The distribution of gains, even where the game can clearly be shown to be non zero-sum, is a legitimate political issue.

However, new arrangements are being introduced in an attempt to ameliorate these academic problems. These arrangements cover trade, investment and debt. Countertrade in all its variants is becoming more widely practised as a second-best solution to trading difficulties such as shortages of foreign exchange amongst less developed countries. More flexible forms of investment involving local participation and non-equity arrangements are attempts to increase the resource flow to LDCs (particularly of technology and management skills) while keeping foreign control at politically manageable levels. Many innovative solutions are being sought to the problem of debt, although it has to be said that these involve rescuing the international banks as well as (or indeed instead of) the debtor nations. The phenomenon of South–South cooperation is also increasingly manifested in the transfer of technology, capital and skills amongst less developed countries, and the study of these flows remains a useful activity.

In raising these issues, a rather fundamental problem re-emerges. It is, simply: what is a developing or less developed country? Clearly Ethiopia is different from Singapore. Essentially development studies is still suffering from the 1960s concept that all poor countries need Western aid. A fresh theoretical concept is needed. Such a concept must incorporate the notion that countries differ not only in resource endowments but also in their historical trajectories. Basic differences sustain these trajectories which arise from deep-seated cultural differences. A mode of analysis which relies solely on comparing comparative static results cannot capture these evolutionary dynamics.

6. The analysis of joint ventures, alliances and cooperative forms of international business activities

Much of the recent development in international business theories has been in the area which is an interface between firm and market. One major development has been the need to classify and name various forms of business activity not previously separately distinguished. Unfortunately this has often led to confusion, double counting, overlapping definitions and the creation of empty boxes. This confusion results from the lack of a set of analytical tools to do the job in hand. Distinctions are only useful when exclusive categories can be created with unique and ultimately measurable dimensions.

The collection edited by Contractor and Lorange (1988) is an excellent example of the work done in this area. A great deal of careful and extensive empirical work has taken place in the classification of cooperative ventures, in examining the motivations of the participants and the external circumstances surrounding the creation of joint ventures and other cooperative modes. Perhaps less attention has been given to the nature of cooperation itself (Buckley and Casson 1988) and its role in a competitive economy. The contrast and possible coexistence of these forms of coordination will continue to be an important focus of research interest. The move from static comparisons of markets and hierarchies (or markets, hierarchies and alliances if a third discrete mode can be identified) to a study of dynamic trajectories is likely to focus attention for some time.

The importance of joint ventures is that they encompass elements of cooperative behaviour. The essence of cooperation is trust (Buckley and Casson 1988) and trust can best be analysed within a cultural context. The interplay of cultural forces with organisational innovations such as joint ventures and other cooperative modes of doing business is a key advance of modern international business theory.

7. Studies of international service industries

As in the case of 'new forms' of international operation, one of the major tasks of researchers in the service industries is to define the meaning and scope of services. This has proved difficult and somewhat tortuous.

The importance accorded to the study of service industries is illustrated by the 1988 publication of the United Nations Centre on Transnational Corporations (UNCTC) study *Transnational Corporations in World Development: Trends and Prospects* which devotes nearly 150 pages to 'Transnational Corporations in Services'. While it is an interesting avenue of research and an extension of the traditional province of enquiry of international business researchers, is the study of services likely to extend our theoretical understanding of international business and the multinational enterprise?

The answer appears to be affirmative, but only mildly so. To some extent, all that is involved is a change of emphasis. The service element in manufacturing has arguably been underrated. The distinction between hardware (equipment-related) and software (user services, ability to use the hardware) is appropriate to the distinction between manufacture and service industries. They are clearly interdependent. Linkages between the two often necessitate the provision of a service as an essential counterpart to the production (and indeed, consumption) of a good.

The internationalisation of banks, advertising agencies, accountancy firms, hotels, construction companies and management consultancies, to name a few, has given empirical impetus to the study of service multinationals (Enderwick 1989). Theoretical structures have not been unduly shaken by this new phase of foreign investment. International banks and other service multinationals have been shown to be efficient utilisers of information which can earn a return on a global basis, just as can technological advances. In this they have much in common with Japanese general trading companies (Sogo Shosha) (Buckley 1985). Several firms have been 'pulled' abroad by their clients' internationalisation. But this is no different to firms insisting that their major suppliers follow them abroad – a phenomenon noted long ago. Location-dependent services clearly have to be performed *in situ* and, like extractive multinationals, they have to become multinationals where economies of scale dictate international expansion. On-the-spot contact with clients can here be equated with raw-material deposits!

It is essential to go further and to probe the nature of service industries. It is at least arguable that a distinction can be made between labour-intensive, essentially manual services such as catering against information-intensive services. Information-intensive services have an important cultural dimension. Trade in information services alters societies and organisations in profound ways. Such trade speeds up the transmission of cultural values and attitudes and can play a key role in development processes.

In summary, the danger with service multinationals is that a special case of the general theory of multinationals will be elevated as a rival theory. In this way, service multinationals become identified as 'non-traditional', i.e. non research-intensive multinationals (which many of them are clearly not if 'research' is broadly interpreted). This will be to recreate an old and unnecessary diversion (Buckley 1983, 1988). However, the study of service multinationals can yield a great deal of insight into theories of international business. It is unlikely of itself to lead to fundamentally new theoretical approaches, although changes of emphasis may occur through the study of the development of (particularly) information-intensive services.

CONCLUSION

The development of international business research has led to nothing less than a new agenda for social science research. Its natural development has led away from 'number-crunching' and comparison of comparative static equilibrium results to evolutionary dynamics. The role of cultural differences in producing different trajectories is now at the forefront of the research agenda.

International business research has been vibrant over recent years and so it remains. New conceptual frameworks have emerged. From these frameworks, analytical tools have been created which enable the framework to become tractable in the sense of enabling diffuse information to be meaningfully organised. At the moment there is a sense of disorder, even disintegration, as the research framework becomes more interdisciplinary, all-embracing and even dangerously complicated. However, there are already signs that reintegration is taking place around a stronger, more coherent framework which is able to incorporate non-traditional variables (such as culture and cooperation). It is necessary for researchers to keep an open mind to concepts which may appear to be peripheral to their traditional field of vision. However, these concepts must be incorporated with rigour, and the judicious use of Occam's razor should not be forgotten. It is essential that the grafting of new concepts should occur on to a solid core. We must beware of excessive eclecticism as well as narrow-mindedness.

Notes

1. Matthew 7: 24–7
2. United Nations Centre on Transnational Corporations (1988) *Transnational Corporations in World Development: Trends and Prospects* New York UNCTC.

References

Adler, Nancy J., Nigel Campbell and Andrew Laurent. 1989. 'In search of appropriate methodology: from outside the People's Republic of China looking in', *Journal of International Business Studies*, Spring, 1: 61–74.
Babbage, Charles. 1832. *On the Economy of Machinery and Manufactures* (London: Charles Knight).
Boddewyn, Jean J. 1988. 'Political aspects of MNE theory', *Journal of International Business Studies*, Fall, 3: 341–64.
Briskin, Richard W. 1986. 'The wording and translation of research instruments', in Lonner and Berry (eds), op. cit.
Buckley, Peter J. 1983. 'New theories of international business: some unresolved issues', in Mark Casson (ed.), *The Growth of International Business* (London: George Allen & Unwin).
Buckley, Peter J. 1985. 'The economic analysis of the multinational enterprise: Reading versus Japan', *Hitotsubashi Journal of Economics*, December, 2: 117–24.
Buckley Peter J. 1988. 'The limits of explanation: testing the internalisation theory of the multinational enterprise', *Journal of International Business Studies*, Summer 2: 181–93.
Buckley, Peter J. and Mark Casson. 1976. *The Future of the Multinational Enterprise* (London: Macmillan).

Buckley, Peter J. and Mark Casson. 1985. *The Economic Analysis of the Multinational Enterprise: selected papers* (London: Macmillan).

Buckley, Peter J. and Mark Casson. 1988. 'A theory of co-operation in international business, in Farok J. Contractor and Peter Lorange (eds), *Co-operative Strategies in International Business* (Lexington MA: Lexington Books).

Buckley, Peter J. and Mark Casson. 1989. 'Multinational enterprises in less developed countries: cultural and economic interactions', University of Reading Discussion Papers in International Investment and Business Studies, No. 126, January (forthcoming in Buckley and Clegg 1990).

Buckley, Peter J. and Jeremy Clegg (eds). 1990. *Multinational Enterprises in Less Developed Countries* (London: Macmillan).

Buckley, Peter J., C. L. Pass and Kate Prescott. 1988. 'Measures of international competitiveness: A critical survey', *Journal of Marketing Management*, Winter 2: 175–200.

Buckley, Peter J., C. L. Pass and Kate Prescott. 1990. 'Measures of international competitiveness: empirical results', *Journal of Marketing Management* (forthcoming).

Campbell, Donald T. 1970. 'Techniques for determining cultural biases in comparative research', in Etzioni and DuBow (eds), op cit.

Casson, Mark. 1979. *Alternatives to the Multinational Enterprise* (London: Macmillan)

Casson, Mark. 1985. 'Multinationals and intermediate product trade', in Buckley and Casson, op cit.

Casson, Mark. 1988a. 'The theory of international business as a unified social science', University of Reading Discussion Papers in International Investment and Business Studies, No. 123, November.

Casson, Mark. 1988b. 'Entrepreneurial culture as a competitive advantage', University of Reading Discussion Papers in International Investment and Business Studies, No. 124, November.

Caves, Richard E. 1971. 'International corporations: the industrial economics of foreign investment', *Economica* (New Series) 1:1–27.

Coase, Ronald H. 1937. 'The nature of the firm', *Economica* (New Series) 4: 386–405.

Contractor, Farok J. and Peter Lorange (eds). 1988. *Cooperative Strategies in International Business* (Lexington MA: Lexington Books).

Dunning, John H. 1989. 'The study of international business: a plea for a more interdisciplinary approach'. University of Reading Discussion Papers in International Investment and Business Studies, No. 127, February.

Durkheim, Emile. 1915. *The Elementary Forms of the Religious Life: a study in religious sociology*. Translated by Joseph Ward Swan (London: George Allen & Unwin).

Durkheim, Emile. 1964. *The Division of Labour in Society*, translated by George Simpson (New York: Free Press).

Enderwick, Peter. 1989. *Multinational Service Firms* (London: Routledge).

Ethier, Wilfred J. 1986. 'The multinational firm', *Quarterly Journal of Economics*, November 4: 805–83.

Etzioni, Amitai and Frederic L. DuBow, (eds). 1970. *Comparative Perspectives: theories and methods* (Boston: Little, Brown and Comapny).

Gray, Mark. 1989. 'Marginal obsessions', *Times Higher Education Supplement*, 28 July, p. 9.

Helpman, Elhanan. 1984. 'A simple theory of international trade with multinational corporations'. *Journal of Political Economy*, June 3: 451–71.

Helpman, Elhanan and Paul Krugman. 1985. *Market Structure and Foreign Trade* (Cambridge, Mass., MIT Press).

Horstmann, Ignatius J. and James R. Markusen. 1989. 'Firm specific assets and the gains from direct foreign investment', *Economica* (New Series) February, 1: 41–8.

Kaldor, N. 1934. 'The equilibrium of the firm', *Economic Journal*, March.

Knight, Frank H. 1935. *The Ethics of Competition and other essays* (London: George Allen & Unwin).

Krugman, Paul. 1983. 'The new theories of international trade and the multinational enterprise', in Charles P. Kindleberger and David Audretch (eds), *The Multinational Corporation in the 1980s* (Cambridge Mass.: MIT Press).

Lonner, Walter J. and John W. Berry, (eds). 1986. *Field Methods in Cross Cultural Research* (Beverly Hills: Sage Publications).

Markusen, James R. 1981. 'Trade and the gains from trade with imperfect competition'. *Journal of International Economics*.

Markusen, James R. 1984. 'Multinationals, multi-plant economies and the gains from trade', *Journal of International Economics*, 205–26.

Phillips, Herbert P. 1970. 'Problems of translation and meaning in field work', in Etzioni and DuBow, (eds), op. cit.

Rokkan, Stein. 1970. 'Recent developments in cross-national research', in Etzioni and DuBow (eds), op. cit.

Rugman, Alan M. 1986. 'New theories of the multinational enterprise: an assessment of internalisation theory', *Bulletin of Economic Research* 2: 101–18.

Schumpeter, J. A. 1934. *The Theory of Economic Development* (Cambridge, Mass.: Harvard University Press).

Smith, Adam. 1776. *An Inquiry into the Nature and Causes of the Wealth of Nations* (ed. R. H. Campbell, A. S. Skinner and W. B. Todd) (Oxford: Clarendon Press, 1976).

Toynbee, Arnold. 1953. *The World and the West: BBC Reith Lectures 1952* (Oxford: Oxford University Press).

Toyne, Brian. 1989. 'International exchange: a foundation for theory building in international business', *Journal of International Business Studies*, Spring, 1: 1–18.

United Nations Center on Transnational Corporations. 1988. *Transnational Corporations in World Development: trends and prospects* (New York: UNCTC).

Weber, Max. 1923. *General Economic History*, translated by Frank H. Knight (London: George Allen & Unwin).

Weber, Max. 1930. *The Protestant Ethic and the Spirit of Captitalism*, translated by Talcott Parsons (London: George Allen & Unwin).

Weber, Max. 1947. *The Theory of Social and Economic Organisation*, translated by A. N. Henderson and Talcott Parsons (New York: Oxford University Press).

Weber, Max. 1949. *The Methodology of the Social Sciences*, translated by Edward A. Shils and Henry A. Finch (New York: Free Press).

Weber, Max. 1965. *The Sociology of Religion*, translated by Ephraim Fischoff, 4th edition, revised by Johannes Wickelmann (London: Methuen).

3 Multinational Enterprises in Less Developed Countries: Cultural and Economic Interactions

Peter J. Buckley and Mark Casson

3.1 INTRODUCTION

This chapter analyses the operations of multinational enterprises (MNEs) in less developed countries (LDCs) in terms of the interplay between two types of culture. The MNE, it is claimed, personifies the highly entrepreneurial culture of the source country, while the LDC personifies the less entrepreneurial culture of the typical social group in the host country. This view places MNE–LDC relations in an appropriate historical perspective. It is the entrepreneurial culture of the source country which explains why in the past that country had the economic dynamism to become a developed country (DC). Conversely, the limited entrepreneurial culture of the host country explains why it has been so economically static that it has remained an LDC. The current problems perceived by MNEs in operating in certain LDCs – and also the problems perceived by these LDCs with the operation of foreign MNEs – reflect the difficulties of attempting to bridge this cultural gap.

The concept of entrepreneurial culture is, of course, related to the concept of 'modernisation' which appears in the sociology of development (Eisenstadt 1973; Herskovits 1961; Inkeles and Smith 1974). There are important differences, however. The concept of entrepreneurial culture derives from economic theories of the entrepreneur (Hayek 1937; Kirzner 1973; Knight 1921; Schumpeter 1934) which identify specific functions such as arbitrage, risk-bearing and innovation needed for economic development. It describes the cultural values which stimulate the emergence of individual personalities capable of performing these functions competently. Modernisation, on the other hand, typically begins with a wide range of attitudes associated with Western industrial societies, and examines how far these attitudes have permeated LDCs. Entrepreneurial theory suggests that not only are some 'modern' attitudes irrelevant to economic development, but others are actually inimical to it. Emphasis on entrepreneurial culture does not therefore imply a trite endorsement of 'modern' values. Entrepreneurial theory has been applied to development issues by a number of writers – Hagen (1962), Hoselitz (1961), Kilby (1971) and McClelland and Winter (1969), for example – but along rather different lines.

Countries classified as LDCs form an extremely heterogeneous group. Indeed, differences between the poorest and the wealthiest LDCs are in some respects greater than between the wealthiest LDCs and many DCs. This chapter is concerned principally with the poorest and most persistently underdeveloped LDCs – such as some countries of sub-Saharan Africa. Since these countries are, generally speaking, the ones with the lowest MNE involvement, it may be asked why a focus on these countries is appropriate. One reason is that this low involvement itself merits explanation, since the continuing confinement of these countries to the periphery of the world economy is of considerable policy interest (Wallerstein 1979). By examining the difficulties encountered by the small number of MNEs that actually invest in these countries, the lack of interest of the majority can be explained in terms of their rational perception of the size of the problem. The second reason is that the starker contrast between wealthy DCs and the poorest LDCs reveals cultural influences in a sharper relief.

Levels of development can vary not only across LDCs but also across regions within any one of them. This point is fully recognised by the analysis in this chapter, which emphasises that regional differences in development are endemic in DCs as well (Berger and Piore 1980). The difference between urban (especially metropolitan) and rural areas is fundamental in this respect. Indeed the analysis below suggests that many international differences in levels of development can be ascribed to differences in the relative influence of urban as opposed to rural culture.

Multinationals differ too; in the present context, differences between source countries are likely to be most significant because these affect the national culture upon which the headquarters of the firm draws. There can also be differences between firms from the same country due, for example, to the religious affiliations of the founders, or the impact of the size of the firm on its organisation and leadership style. Due to limited space, however, this chapter abstracts from such considerations by working with the concept of a representative MNE.

Section 2 delineates the main areas in which conventional economic theory appears to be deficient in explaining MNE behaviour in LDCs. The 'residual' phenomena which remain unexplained by economic factors, it is suggested, may be explicable by cultural factors instead. The analytical core of the chapter comprises sections 3–7. These sections consider in detail the interaction between geographical and cultural factors in the process of development. Section 3 identifies three conditions for successful economic development; one is geographical – entrepôt potential – and two are cultural – a scientific outlook, and a commitment to voluntary methods of social and economic coordination. Sections 4–6 elaborate on each of these factors in turn, generating a checklist of country characteristics relevant to economic development. Section 7 draws on the core analysis to expound an evolutionary model of world development, which focuses on the dynamics of the linkages between DCs and LDCs, as mediated by MNEs. Section 8 returns to the key issues identified in section 2. It explains how difficulties faced by some LDCs in learning new technologies originate in specific cultural factors, and urges that these same cultural factors explain other phenomena too. Attention is drawn to the weaknesses as well as the strengths of contemporary entrepreneurial cultures, and it is suggested that some of the cultural values transmitted by MNEs to LDCs hinder rather than help the process of development. Section 9 concludes the paper with suggestions for further research.

3.2 KEY ISSUES

Any analysis of multinational operations in LDCs must address a number of key stylised facts. Some of these facts are readily explained by conventional economic theory (see, for example, Casson and Pearce 1987), but others are not. The facts that conventional theory can explain include:

(1) *The limited scale and disappointing economic performance of import-substituting manufacturing investments in LDCs.* This is partly attributable to inappropriate LDC trade policies. By protecting relatively small domestic markets for finished manufactures, LDC governments have encouraged the proliferation of downstream assembly-type operations of less than efficient scale. It is only the ability to charge monopoly prices well above world export prices that has encouraged MNEs to continue operating in these protected markets.

(2) *The increase in foreign divestments since the oil price shocks of the mid-1970s* is partly explained by the reduction in real consumer incomes in oil-exporting LDCs, which has reduced local demand for relatively sophisticated MNE-produced goods. The threat of blocked profit repatriations from countries with balance of payments difficulties has also encouraged a pre-emptive liquidation of foreign investments by MNEs.

(3) *The recent poor performance of resource-based investments in Africa*

and Latin America is partly explained by another consequence of the oil price shocks – namely the recession in Western heavy industries – and by the continuing protection of domestic agriculture in industrial societies. It is also due partly to the development of new mineral deposits in the Asia-Pacific region. Finally, the emergence of synthetic substitutes has reduced the long-term demand for certain minerals (although the price advantage of oil-based substitutes has declined).

(4) *The use of capital-intensive technologies by MNEs in labour-abundant LDCs* can be explained partly by the cost of adapting to local conditions a technology originally developed for use in Western locations. It can also be explained by the importance of mechanisation in meeting quality standards in export markets – and in home markets dominated by wealthy consumers (in countries with a highly-skewed distribution of income). The distortion of factor prices in LDC markets through minimum wage legislation, capital subsidies, and so on may also be significant.

Some of the salient points which existing theory cannot easily explain are:

(5) *The failure of techhnology transfer to generate sustained innovative capability in LDC industries.* The much slower rate at which foreign technologies are assimilated by the poorest LDCs compared to newly-industrialising countries such as South Korea, or successfully industrialised countries such as Japan, suggests that cultural factors may inhibit the acquisition of scientific ideas and Western working practices.

(6) *The confinement of modern industry to 'enclaves', and in particular the failure of foreign investors to develop backward linkages with indigenous suppliers.* Where resource-based investments are concerned, there may be limited opportunities for backward linkages in any case. Even in developed countries, furthermore, large-scale investments often fail to develop a local supply base; the disciplined routine of work in large plants seems to inhibit the 'incubation' of entrepreneurial skills in the local workforce. Nevertheless, the frequent claim by MNE managers of medium-size manufacturing operations that the quality of local supplies is persistently deficient suggests that there may be a systematic failure in LDCs to appreciate the importance of component quality and of precision work in manufacturing industries.

(7) *Poor internal relations, both between headquarters and subsidiary, and between management and labour within the foreign subsidiary.* Conflicts between different groups within the firm over the distribution of profit, the level of investment, and so on, are common in any business activity, and there may be special reasons – such as the high risks perceived by foreign investors and their consequently short-term perspective on cash flow – why these conflicts may be particularly acute in respect of LDC

operations. Nevertheless, it is also possible that the failure to resolve these conflicts effectively is due to frequent misunderstandings caused by cross-cultural barriers to communication.

(8) *The tendency for industrialisation through foreign technology to precipitate the disintegration of traditional social groups within the host economy.* All innovation does, of course, involve 'creative destruction', but the social groups of developing countries seem to be much more vulnerable in this respect than do equivalent social groups in the developed world.

It is worth noting that even the 'successful' explanations in (1)–(4) involve only the most proximate causes of the effects involved. Thus in respect of (1), for example, it is possible to ask the more fundamental question of why so many LDC governments opted for protectionism in the first place. Were they susceptible to economic analysis supporting import-substitution because they were predisposed to break economic as well as social and political ties with their colonial powers in order to bolster independence? It seems that – in this case at least – the more fundamental are the questions asked, and the further back the quest for explanation goes, the more likely are cultural factors to become significant.

A good theory often has the capacity to explain more than was originally asked of it, and it is claimed that this is also true of the analysis presented here. The theory can explain not only contemporary differences between DCs and LDCs, but also certain aspects of the historical process of indus-trialisation in countries which have become DCs. Thus the vulnerability of traditional social groups, for example, noted above, applies also to the social groups which became extinct a century or more ago during the industrialisation of DCs. There is insufficient space in the present chapter, however, to document all the relevant facts, let alone substantiate the claim of the theory to explain them.

3.3 THE PROCESS OF DEVELOPMENT

A necessary condition for development in any locality is that there are resources with a potential for exploitation. Conventional economic theory tends to underestimate the obstacles that lie in the path of realising this potential, however. Working with traditional concepts of resource endow-ment – land, labour and capital – cross-section regressions using the total factor productivity approach have only limited success in explaining inter-national differences in material economic performance (as measured by per capita GNP) (Pack 1987). Some countries clearly underperform by failing to realise their potential, and the question is why this should be so (Leibenstein 1978).

Differences in education and training are commonly cited as a possible explanation, and the analysis presented here is generally consistent with this view. It goes beyond it, however, in recognising that education takes place largely outside formal institutions. Early education, in particular, is effected through family influence, peer group pressure within the local community, and so on. To benefit fully from formal education it may be necessary for people to 'unlearn' beliefs from their informal education. But if the conflict between the two sets of beliefs is acute then psychological obstacles to unlearning may arise. Measures of educational input based on gross expenditure fail to capture these important factors. The analysis in this chapter helps to identify those aspects of the formal curriculum which are crucial in supporting economic development. It also identifies those elements of general culture which prepare people to benefit from such education.

Two main obstacles to the efficient use of national resources can be identified. The first is geographical: the inability to effect a division of labour due to obstacles to transportation. In this context, it is argued below

TABLE 3.1 *Factors in the long-run economic success of a nation*

I. Geographical factors that influence entrepôt potential.
  A Location near to major long-distance freight transport routes.
  B Natural harbour with inland river system.
  C Extensive coastline.
  D Land and climate suitable for an agriculture with potential for local
     downstream processing.
  E Mineral deposits and energy resources.

II. Entrepreneurial culture.
  Technical aspects.
  A Scientific attitude, including a systems view.
  B Judgemental skills, including
     (i) ability to simplify
     (ii) self-confidence
     (iii) detached perception of risk
     (iv) understanding of delegation
  Moral aspects
  C Voluntarism and toleration.
  D Association with trust, including
     (i) general commitment to principles of honesty, stewardship,
      and the like
     (ii) sense of corporate mission
     (iii) versatile personal bonding (friendship not confined to kin)
     (iv) weak attachments to specific locations, roles, and so on.
  E High norms in respect of effort, quality of work, accumulation of wealth,
    social distinction, and so on.

---

that the presence of a potential entrepôt centre is crucial in facilitating the development of a region. The second is the absence of an entrepreneurial culture. An entrepreneurial culture provides an economy with flexibility – in particular, the structural flexibility to cope with changes in the division of labour. These changes may be progressive changes stemming from essentially autonomous technological innovations, or defensive changes made in response to resource depletion or various environmental disturbances.

An entrepreneurial culture has two main aspects: the technical and the moral (see Table 3.1). The technical aspect stimulates the study of natural laws through experimentation, and the assimilation of technologies developed by other cultures too. It also develops judgemental skills in decision-making – skills that are particularly important in simplifying complex situations without unduly distorting perceptions of them (Casson 1988b).

Entrepreneurial opportunities are usually best exploited through contracts, organisation-building, and other forms of association. The moral aspect involves a grasp of the principles involved in voluntary associations of this kind. These principles include commitments to honesty, stewardship, and other values that underpin contractual arrangements of both a formal and informal nature. They also include a concept of group mission which is needed to mitigate agency problems in large organisations. A willingness to trust people other than kin is also important. Finally, there must be no rigid attachments to specific occupational roles or places of residence which can inhibit social or geographical mobility at times when structural adjustments are required.

It is worth stressing the diversity of the elements embraced by this moral aspect. Some of these elements have recently been eroded within Western industrial societies (Hirsch 1977). These societies – notably the US – have developed an extreme competitive individualism, in which levels of trust are inefficiently low. The level of trust required for successful voluntary association is more likely to be present in countries with sophisticated traditional cultures that have recently been modernised – such as Japan.

It is useful to distinguish between high-level entrepreneurship, as exemplified by Schumpeter's heroic vision of system-wide innovation, and low-level entrepreneurship of the kind undertaken by petty traders in small market towns, which can be analysed using the Austrian concepts of arbitrage and market process. High-level entrepreneurship generally requires all the elements of entrepreneurial culture itemised in Table 3.1, while low-level entrepreneurship requires only some – it depends principally on good judgement, and to some extent on the absence of attachments that impede mobility. It is this contrast between high-level and low-level entrepreneurship – rather than the presence or absence of entrepreneurship – which seems to be important in explaining the difference between DCs and LDCs. In other words, it is a relative and not an absolute difference with which the analysis is concerned.

Geographical and cultural factors are linked because the geography of a territory can influence the kind of culture that emerges within it. This is because geographical impediments to communication reduce personal mobility and partition a country into small isolated social groups. Internal coordination within these groups tends to rely on primitive mechanisms of reciprocity and the like which depend crucially on stability of membership (Casson 1988a, b). As explained below, the cultures of these groups are likely to emphasise conformity and coercion rather than individuality and choice, and so inhibit spontaneous entrepreneurial activity.

Good communications, on the other hand, provide opportunities for appropriating gains from interregional trade. Groups that inhabit areas with good communications will tend to prosper, provided their leaders adopt a tolerant attitude towards entrepreneurial middlemen who promote trade. Groups which develop an entrepreneurial culture will tend to expand the geographical scope of their operations (through commercially-inspired voyages of discovery, and so on). Technological advances in transportation will be encouraged because their liberal policies permit the appropriation of material rewards by inventors and innovators. Geographical expansion eventually brings these groups into contact with isolated groups who occupy resource-rich locations. These locations would be inaccessible without the transportation technology and logistical skills of the entrepreneurial group. Equipped with superior technology, the entrepreneurial group can, if its leaders wish, subdue the isolated groups by military means. Different entrepreneurial groups may become rivals in pre-empting opportunities for the exploitation of overseas resources. This may lead to military conflict between the groups, or to a compromise solution where each group maintains its own economic empire and political sphere of influence.

The creation of a transport infrastructure within these hitherto isolated territories not only gives access to resources (and incidentally improves imperial defence);it also tends to undermine the viability of indigenous cultures. Ease of transportation promotes personal mobility and so destroys the stability of membership on which the local groups' methods of internal coordination depend. The confrontation between MNEs and LDCs can be understood as one aspect of this final phase in which the technologies of the entrepreneurial societies are transferred to the regions occupied by the hitherto isolated social groups. To fully understand the nature of this confrontation, however, it is necessary to study in detail the various aspects of the process of development outlined above.

3.4 GEOGRAPHICAL DETERMINANTS OF ENTREPÔT POTENTIAL

A division of labour creates a system of functionally specialised elements. The elements which consitute the system have complementary roles. The division of labour is normally effected over space. Different activities are concentrated at different locations and are connected by intermediate product flows. A large system typically comprises interrelated subsystems, and usually the subsystems themselves can be further decomposed.

System operation over space depends on ease of transportation, and in this context the existence of low-cost facilities for the bulk movement of intermediate products is crucial.

Water transport has significant cost advantages for the bulk movement of freight, and this implies that a good river system and a long coastline (in relation to land area) are an advantage. These conditions are most likely to be satisfied by an island or peninsula with low-lying terrain. Water transport is, however, vulnerable through icing, flooding, and the like, and so geological features that facilitate road and rail construction are also useful.

Good transportation expands the area of the market for the final output of each process. It permits a much finer division of labour because economies of scale in individual plants can be exploited more effectively. In general, steady expansion of the market permits the evolution of system structure. The horizontal division of labour expands to proliferate varieties of final product whilst the vertical division of labour extends to generate a larger number of increasingly simple (and hence more easily mechanised and automated) stages of production.

The development of a region depends not only on the progress of its internal division of labour, but also on its ability to participate in a wider division of labour beyond its boundaries. The external division of labour (as traditional trade theory emphasises) allows the region to specialise in those activities which make the most intensive use of the resources with which it is relatively best endowed.

The interface between the internal and external division of labour is typically an entrepôt centre. Whether or not a region includes a location with entrepôt potential will exert a significant influence on its development (Hodges 1988). The general advantages of water transport, noted earlier, are reflected in the fact that the cost of long-distance bulk transportation is normally lowest by sea. This means that port facilities are normally necessary for successful entrepôt operation. Since ships afford significant economies of scale in their construction and operation a successful port must be designed to handle large sea-going (and ocean-going) vessels.

A port located close to major international and intercontinental shipping routes may become an important node on a global network of trade. Port activities will comprise both the transhipment of bulk consignments on connecting trunk routes and also 'break bulk' and 'make bulk' operations geared to local feeder services. In this context, the location of the port on the estuary of an extensive river system is advantageous. A centre of transhipment and consolidation is, moreover, a natural place at which to carry out processing activities. Handling costs are reduced because goods can be unloaded directly into the processing facility from the feeder systems, and then later loaded directly from the processing facility on to the trunk system (or vice versa).

The need for processing exported goods depends upon the type of agricultural and mineral production undertaken in the hinterland of the port. In the pre-industrial phase of port development, agricultural processing is likely to be particularly significant. Now crops such as corn and barley offer relatively limited opportunities for downstream processing before consumption – baking and brewing being respectively the main activities concerned – while rice feeds into even fewer activities. Animal production, by contrast, generates dairy products, meat and hides, while hides, in turn, feed into the leather and clothing sequence. Sheep are particularly prolific in generating forward linkages, as their wool feeds into the textile sequence. The textile sequence is simple to mechanise and has the capacity to produce a wide range of differentiated fashion products. (Cotton feeds into a similar sequence, but unlike sheep does not generate meat and hides as well.) The potential for forward linkages varies dramatically, therefore, from rice growing at one extreme to sheep farming on the other.

The location of the processing at the port depends, of course, on it being cheaper to locate the processing in the exporting rather than the importing country. This requirement is generally satisfied by both agricultural and mineral products. The perishability of agricultural products means the processing is usually done as close to the source as possible. Mineral products, though durable, lose weight during processing, and so to minimise transport costs it is usually efficient to process close to the source as well.

Mineral processing is, however, energy-intensive, and energy sources, such as fossil fuels, are often even more expensive to transport than mineral ores themselves. The absence of local energy resources can therefore lead to the relocation of processing away from the exporting country. Mineral processing can also generate hazardous by-products. Access to a coastline near the port where such by-products can be dumped is important, therefore, if minerals are to be processed before export.

While the processing of imported products is likely to be of much less economic significance, for reasons implicit in the discussion above, there are a few exceptions. Imports from an LDC, for example, may well arrive in a raw state, because of the lack of suitable energy supplies or labour skills in the exporting country. Furthermore, the more sophisticated are consumer tastes in the importing country, the more extensive is the processing that is likely to be required. Thus the greater the gap in development between the exporting and importing country, the more likely it is that the amount of value-added in import-processing will be significant.

The agglomeration of activities within a port provides an opportunity for exploiting economies of scale in the provision of defence, law and order, drainage and sewage systems, and so on. It also provides a large local market which promotes the development of highly specialised services – not only commercial services, but also consumer services – of the kind that could never be provided in country areas with dispersed populations. (Such economies of urbanisation can, of course, be provided without a port, and many countries do, in fact, contain inland administrative capitals which support such services. The viability of such capitals often depends, however, on cross-subsidisation from tax revenues generated at an entrepôt centre, and the social benefits derived from them may therefore be imputed to entrepôt activity.)

It is sometimes claimed that, contrary to the argument above, entrepôt devoted to the bulk export of agricultural products and raw materials are inherently enclavistic. The crucial question here is how fast the linkages between the entrepôt and the village communities of the hinterland develop. In the history of Western DCs provincial agricultural marketing and light manufacturing have grown up in medium-sized towns whose merchants intermediate between the village and the entrepôt. Even in LDCs with limited rural transport infrastructure, the tentacles of trade can extend to the village in respect of livestock farming because livestock can be driven to market over distances that are prohibitive so far as the carriage of crops is concerned. It is, therefore, only if rural culture is strongly opposed to merchant activity that the entrepôt is likely to remain an enclave indefinitely.

The conditions most favourable to industrialisation, it may be concluded, are the existence of a natural habour close to major shipping routes, good internal communications between the port and its hinterland, livestock farming in the hinterland, abundant endowments of both minerals and primary energy sources, and a coastline suitable for the disposal of pollutants. These considerations alone go some way towards explaining both the early industrialisation of temperate-climate, mineral-rich island countries with coastal deposits of fossil fuels, and good inland river systems, such as the

United Kingdom, and their relative decline once their minerals and fossil fuels have been depleted and their comparative advantage in livestock farming has been undermined by the development of overseas territories.

3.5 SCIENTIFIC OUTLOOK AND SYSTEMS THINKING

A territory with entrepôt potential can find its development inhibited by an unsuitable culture. Cultural constraints inhibit entrepreneurship both directly, by discouraging individual initiative, and indirectly by encouraging political leaders to distort incentives and over-regulate the economy.

In some societies the absence of a scientific outlook may well be a problem. Western analysts studying LDCs typically perceive this problem as resulting from the absence of any Renaissance or Enlightenment. The society has not gone through an intellectual revolution in which a mystical view of the world gives way to a more realistic one. The society still relies on anthropomorphic explanations of natural processes, interprets unusual but scientifically explicable events as omens and perceives its real-world environment as the centre of a metaphysical cosmos. This emphasis on things as symbols of something beyond inhibits recognition of things as they really are. It discourages the understanding of nature in terms of mechanism and system interdependency.

A realistic systems view of nature does, however, raise philosophical problems of its own, which can be resolved in various ways. A major difficulty is that if man himself, as a part of nature, is pure mechanism, then choice and moral responsibility become simply an illusion caused by lack of self-knowledge. Western liberal thought resolves this problem through Cartesian dualism, in which the moral world of intentional action coexists alongside the physical world of mechanism.

The scientific outlook does not imply, as is sometimes suggested, a completely secular view of the world. Western Christian thought has also embraced dualism by redefining the role of God as the creator and architect of a self-contained universe, rather than as a super-natural force intervening directly through everyday events. The view that man is fashioned in the image of God encourages the idea that man too has creative abilities. Rejection of the view that the earth is the centre of the universe diminishes man's stature and raises that of nature, encouraging the idea that nature is worthy of serious investigation. Man's contact with God can no longer reasonably be maintained through sacrifices offered in anticipation of favours, but it can be sustained in other ways, such as an appreciation of the elegance and simplicity of physical laws which express this design. Man's creative abilities can be used to explore this design through observation and experiment.

The systems view of nature translates readily into a systems view of production. Production involves a system created by man and superimposed on the system of nature, with which it interacts. A systems view of production involves awareness of the principle of the division of labour – in particular, the importance of decomposing complex tasks into simple ones and allocating resources between these tasks according to comparative advantage. The systems view also emphasises that the strong complementarities between different elements of the system make it vulnerable to the failure of any single element and so create a strong demand for quality control.

The close connection between religious beliefs and attitudes to nature means that in countries where mysticism or superstition prevail, a scientific outlook and systems thinking are unlikely to develop. The concept of harnessing nature to control the future is absolute folly to people who believe that the future is already pre-ordained, or is in the personal hands of powerful and arbitrary gods. As a consequence, their ability to assimilate technological know-how will be very low. Awareness of how local operations fit into a global division of labour will be minimal. For example, the idea that system complementarities necessitate continuity of operation, rigorous punctuality, and so forth, will be quite alien to local operatives. Appreciation of the importance of quality control in the manufacture of components and intermediate products will be missing too.

3.6 COMPETITIVE INDIVIDUALISM VERSUS VOLUNTARY ASSOCIATION

The development of a scientific attitude in the West was associated with the rise of individualism. The idea that people are intelligent and purposeful was applied democratically. Intelligence was not something confined to a traditional elite, but a feature of every mature adult. Emphasis on intelligence led to demands for reasoned argument rather than appeal to traditional authority or divine revelation for the legitimation of moral objectives.

Individualism asserts that each person is the best judge of how his own interests are served. He can deal with other individuals as equals, and use his intelligence to safeguard his own interests in his dealings with them. Interference in other people's affairs on paternalistic grounds is unacceptable. Individualism claims that everyone is capable of forming judgements on wider issues too. Since different people have different experiences, no one can assume that their own opinion is necessarily correct, and so toleration of other people's views is required. Differences of opinion over collective activity need to be resolved peacefully, and so in political life commitment to the democratic process is regarded as more important than approval of the outcome of the process.

Four aspects of individualism are worthy of special mention. The first is the alienability of property, which helps to promote markets in both products and labour. The demystification of the world through the emergence of a scientific outlook undermines the view that people impart something of themselves to the things they produce. It breaks the anthropomorphic link between production and use. As the product of labour becomes depersonalised and objectified, it becomes acceptable to alienate it for use by others. Conversely, it becomes acceptable to claim ownership over things one did not produce. So far as natural resources are concerned, they no longer need to be held in common by the territorial group. They can be privately appropriated, giving the owner an incentive to manage them properly and avoid excessive depletion.

The second aspect is freedom of entry (and of exit) which allows individuals to switch between trading partners and between markets without the permission of established authority. Such freedom also implies freedom from statutory regulation of entry too.

Thirdly, respect for contract, and a right of recourse to an independent judiciary for the resolution of contractual disputes, are aspects of individualism which are important in reducing transaction costs.

Finally, an individualist appreciates that multilateral trade is most easily established through separately negotiated bilateral trades in which goods are bought and sold using a medium of exchange. He recognises that currency is useful as a specialised medium of exchange, and that the most convenient currency is the debt of a reputable debtor such as the sovereign or the state. Individualism is therefore tolerant of debt and of the personality cult that surrounds notes and coin that carry the head of the sovereign. It imposes obligations on the debtor, however, to live up to his reputation through self-restraint: in particular he must not debase the currency through over-issue.

A major cultural weakness of LDCs seems to be a lack of individualistic thinking. In the extreme case of a primitive rural economy, the link between production and consumption remains unbroken: individuals consume what they themselves produce, and thereby forgo the gains from trade. In so far as there is a division of labour, it is confined to within a social group. Different activities are coordinated both by relations of reciprocity between individual members and by members' common sense of obligation to the leader. These mechanisms are most effective within small, stable and compact groups, such as the extended family or the village community. In such groups members regularly expect to encounter one another again, offenders quickly acquire a reputation for bad behaviour and can be easily punished by the leader and, indeed, by other members of the group.

A major defect of such coordination mechanisms is that they depend crucially on stability of membership. If it becomes easy for members to quit, then reputations become less valuable, and punishment is easier to evade. Moreover, conditions of geographical isolation, which tend to promote stability of membership, also mean that the threat of expulsion from the group can be very severe. This allows a leader to acquire enormous power over individual members, provided he can 'divide' the members against each other or otherwise prevent them joining forces to overthrow him. Thus while isolation may help to promote close emotional ties between the followers, the leader may be feared rather than respected or loved.

Individualism has its own problems, however, in coordinating the activities of groups. Because individualism promotes inter-group mobility, it not only undermines the 'despotic' solution to intra-group coordination but also the internal reputation mechanism too. A purely competitive form of individualism, which encourages individuals to join teams purely for the material benefits, offers no effective substitute for primitive reciprocity.

When followers' efforts can be easily monitored by the leader there is little problem for competitive individualism, because the material rewards of each member can be linked to his individual performance. When effort becomes difficult to monitor, however, material incentives have to be related to team output, and when the team is large a share of the team bonus may be insufficient to prevent team members slacking. Unless there is a shared sense of corporate mission, individuals are likely to put too little effort into team activity. The leader cannot trust his followers not to slacken. If the leader cannot be trusted either then the followers may not respond to his incentives anyway, because they believe he will default on the agreement if he can get away with it.

Another problem of individualism is that the inalienability of the individual's right to quit may induce higher rates of inter-group mobility than are compatible with efficiency. Successful teamwork often requires members to accumulate on-the-job experience in learning to anticipate each other's actions; unrestricted freedom to enter and exit can allow transitory members who lack this experience to profit at the expense of their colleagues.

Widening the range of an individual's legitimate commitments from mere respect for property and contract to generate trust by instilling a sense of corporate mission significantly modifies the moral basis of individualism.

The resulting philosophy is essentially one of voluntary association. This philosophy retains many of the attributes of competitive individualism, but emphasises that the contract of group membership involves acceptance of discipline imposed by the leader. Freedom exists principally in choosing between alternative group commitments, rather than in maintaining full discretion within the chosen group. It also emphasises that commitment to a group is a source of emotional satisfaction, and that more commitment rather than less may make people better off. It does not attempt to repudiate the 'minimal commitment' of competitive individualism but rather to augment this commitment with others.

Widening the range of commitments creates the possibility of moral conflicts. To a heavily committed individual, indeed, it is the resolution of moral dilemmas that often appears to be the essence of choice. Experience in coping with moral dilemmas of this kind may well improve general decision-making skills.

The global organisation of production implemented by sophisticated MNEs depends crucially upon such commitments to mitigate what would otherwise be insuperable agency problems. However intense the competition between MNEs, within each MNE cooperation between the parent and each subsidiary needs to be maintained at a high level. A clear group mission, articulated by a charismatic business leader who makes an effective role model, can be crucial in this respect.

It is therefore worth noting that the kind of individualism harnessed by the successful MNE is very different from the culture of unrestrained self-assertion – or even exhibitionism – which can be found in many societies, including LDCs. The extrovert 'individualism' of adolescent males, for example, has little connection with the mature individualism of the successful entrepreneur. People who exhibit no self-restraint cannot normally be trusted, and so make poor business risks for financiers, and bad employees. The observation, often heard, that there is 'too much individualism' rather than too little in LDCs, confuses exhibitionism with the mature individualism described above. It is not too much individualism that is the problem but too little individualism of the appropriate kind.

3.7 GEOGRAPHICAL AND CULTURAL ASPECTS OF A GLOBAL TRADING SYSTEM

The preceding analysis suggests that the differences between developed countries (DCs) and LDCs lie not only in resource endowments but in the fact that the territories of the former embrace potential entrepôt centres and that cultural obstacles to the realisation of this potential are relatively weak. An LDC is likely to be a country that has no entrepôt potential, and poor internal communications which make it unlikely to develop an indigenous entrepreneurial culture. A DC, on the other hand, is a country with both entrepôt potential and an entrepreneurial culture.

A country that has entrepôt potential but lacks an indigenous entrepreneurial culture is likely to find that, in the course of time, entrepôt operations emerge under the ownership and control of foreign entrepreneurs based in DCs. These entrepreneurs have the system thinking needed to recognise the entrepôt potential, and are likely to control established international transport and distribution systems into which the new operations can be integrated. The external commercial relations of these countries may become heavily dependent upon an international trading system governed by the requirements of DC markets, and controlled by DC interests, whilst profits generated by entrepôt operations may be repatriated too.

Within any given historical epoch, the process of development begins with the countries that later emerge as the DC investors in LDCs. These countries may subsequently go into decline, but this process of decline is not considered here – it is treated as a separate issue, involving the transition from one historical epoch to another (cf. Wiener 1981).

In modelling the process of development in global terms, the advantages of water transport over land-based transport – emphasised earlier – play an important role. These advantages mean that maritime trade between entrepôt centres in different countries is likely to be of much greater significance for each country than inland trade between the entrepôt and its remoter hinterland. The fortunes of individual countries are therefore closely linked to their place within the world trading system. Another consequence of the dominance of maritime trade is that even DCs may experience a degree of dualism in their development, between the entrepôt centre on the one hand, and the remoter hinterland on the other. A somewhat ironic corollary of this is that the most unfortunate LDCs, which have no valuable resources and no entrepôt potential, may be the only countries not to experience dualism, purely because they have no development either.

A typical sequence of global development is shown in Figures 3.1 and 3.2. There are two phases. The first involves the rise of DCs prompted by the development of trade between them. The second involves the emergence of LDCs and their own subsequent development.

In the first phase (see Figure 3.1) it is assumed that there are two potential DCs, A and B, each of which is initially segmented into isolated social groups which control particular resources (see sector (a)). Resource endowments are denoted by circles, with large endowments that have

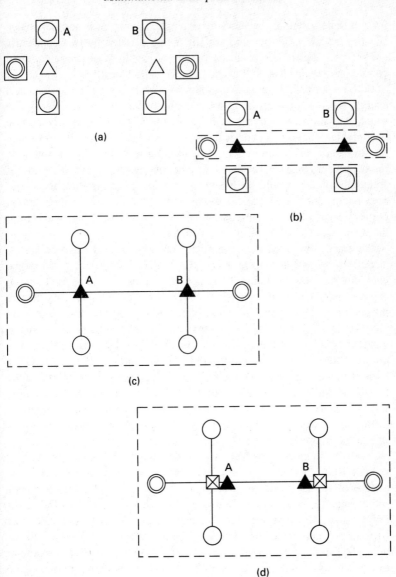

Note: For explanation of symbols, see text.

FIGURE 3.1 *The development of international trade between developed countries*

foreign trade potential (because, for example, the output is non-perishable and has a high value per unit weight) being denoted by two concentric circles. Each square box encloses a group of people who share a common culture and reside close to a given resource endowment.

Both countries have a natural harbour which forms a potential entrepôt centre. The resources all lie in a hinterland which can be accessed given suitable investment in transport infrastructure. The harbour represents a potential entrepôt centre, and is denoted by a white triangle. It is assumed that in each country the indigenous culture around the major resource is reasonably progressive, so that this potential can be realised. A line of communication is established between the groups controlling the major resource of each country, and two-way trade develops through the entrepôt ports. Realisation of the entrepôt potential is indicated by the switch from the white triangle to the black one in sector (b).

The trade flow intensifies communications between the two countries, leading to cultural homogenisation. This is illustrated by the fact that the two countries now lie within the same box – at least so far as the entrepôt centres and the export-oriented hinterlands are concerned. This culture differs from the cultures of the isolated groups in the less promising hinterlands. The trading system strengthens the progressive element in the indigenous culture of the export-oriented hinterland by giving greater emphasis to the individual's right to hold property and his ability to fend for himself in the negotiation of trades. Competition between the port and the hinterland for employees also stimulates a friendlier and less autocratic style of leadership within social groups. This new commercial culture is distinguished from the culture of the isolated groups by the use of a dashed line in the figure.

As each entrepôt centre develops, the advantages of utilising more fully its indivisible facilities – notably the port – encourage the generation of additional feeder traffic by investment in transport links with the less-promising areas of hinterland (see sector (c)). The entrepôt now handles not only additional export traffic, but also inter-regional traffic between different parts of the hinterland. In other words, the entrepôt becomes a hub for domestic freight transport too. Each country becomes homogenised around the commercial culture as a result. This stage of evolution may well be protracted. Many so-called developed countries still contain isolated rural areas where the commercial culture has made limited inroads.

Before this stage has been completed, the fourth stage may begin. This involves processing exports at the port, in order to reduce the bulk and increase the value of long-distance cargo. Downstream processing of this kind is illustrated in the figure by a cross within a square (see sector (d)). Industrialisation around the port will have further cultural consequences, but these are not considered here.

The second phase of the development sequence begins when one of the developed countries, say A, makes contact with an LDC, C. C is still in the situation that A was in at the beginning of the first phase, but with this difference – that C remains undeveloped partly because it has a less progressive culture. Its initial state is illustrated in sector (a) of Figure 3.2. The figure has been simplified by omitting the domestic trade flows within countries A and B.

If A discovers C before B does, A may attempt to monopolise trade with C, so that all trade between B and C has to be routed *via* A. Colonial occupation or control of international shipping lanes may be used to enforce the exclusion of B. So far as C is concerned, it is faced with the impact *via* A, of an established commercial culture which has evolved over a long time from roots which were, in any case, more progressive. This opens up a wide cultural gap within C between the highly commercial imported culture of the entrepôt centre on the one hand and the less-promising areas of hinterland on the other. This is illustrated in sector (c). Cultural dualism impedes the final stage of development, shown in sector (d), where linkages are established with the remaining hinterland. Downstream processing around

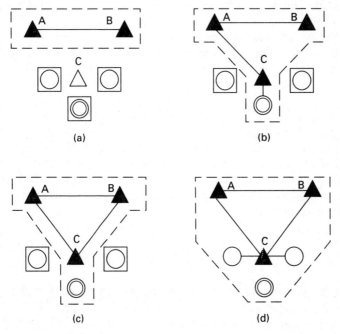

(a) (b)

(c) (d)

FIGURE 3.2 *The role of developed countries in the development of LDCs*

the entrepôt centre may also develop in this final stage, but this is not shown in the figure.

Two main social groups are available to bridge this cultural gap. One is the resident expatriates, who may have moved abroad originally as employees of the MNE or the DC government. The other is the group of indigenous individuals – merchants and other educated people drawn mainly from the middle and upper ranks of the host society – who are quick to take advantage of the profit opportunities from cultural brokerage. They are willing to learn the language and customs, and adopt the style of dress, of the DC – and perhaps send their children to be educated there as well – in order to consolidate their position. The size of these two groups, and their ability to combine forces where necessary, is crucial in determining the spread of entrepôt influence within the DC.

The analysis suggests that while the process of development in an LDC is similar in outline to that previously followed by an established DC, there are three important differences, which arise chiefly because the LDC is a latecomer to development.

First, the reason why it is a latecomer is partly that it has an unprogressive culture. There may be considerable resistance to the development of entrepôt activity, and indigenous entrepreneurs may be so slow off the mark that foreigners dominate the operations. There may even be political support for a policy of closing the harbour to foreign merchants.

Secondly, if the entrepôt centre is opened up under colonial rule, foreign merchants may enjoy significant market power. Thus few of the gains of trade that accrued to the developed country in the early stages of its own development may accrue to the LDC as it passes through a similar stage itself.

Thirdly, the LDC is confronted with a very sophisticated trading system organised by developed country trade, and with a matching culture very much at variance with its own. Thus, although superficially it might seem that an LDC should be able to catch up quickly with developed countries, its vulnerability to the exercise of market power and the magnitude of the cultural gap may well cause discrepancies in the level of development to persist for a very long time.

3.8 CULTURAL ASPECTS OF MNE OPERATIONS

The MNE is the major institution through which both the technology and the entrepreneurial culture of the DC is transferred to the LDC economy. The largest and most sophisticated MNEs are based in DCs; they utilise advanced technologies to operate internationally rationalised production systems. Systems thinking is highly developed in the headquarters of these firms. Strategic attitudes to competition are also well developed because of continuing oligopolistic rivalry between MNEs in major DC markets.

The analysis in this chapter shows that there are substantial cultural barriers to disseminating attitudes of this kind to indigenous managers, and to their subordinates, in LDCs. One obvious way of educating local employees is to send out managers from headquarters on short-term overseas appointments. This may encounter difficulties if the location is sufficiently unattractive to Western eyes that managers resist reassignment to the extent that they prefer to resign instead. In any case, these managers may have difficulties communicating with their subordinates, so while headquarters–subsidiary relations may be good, internal relations within the subsidiary may be poor. In some cases resident expatriates may be employed instead, though there is a risk that they will be out of touch with the more sophisticafed ideas developed at headquarters.

An alternative is to hire locally and send recruits to headquarters for extensive training before they return to the subsidiary. Training is, however, likely to be difficult – even at headquarters – unless the local recruits already have some Western-style education, while may well mean that indigenous recruitment is confined to a small social elite. This strategy is inappropriate, moreover, when establishing a new subsidiary; managers will normally have to be sent out from headquarters to organise recruitment, and they can only be replaced when the flow of trained recruits has come on-stream.

Cross-cultural barriers also explain why spillovers from MNE operations in LDCs are so limited. The capacity of indigenous competitors to imitate – let alone adapt or improve upon – imported technologies is limited by their lack of scientific outlook. Similarly, the inability of local firms to emerge as subcontractors competing against imported component supplies stems from their failure to appreciate the importance of precision and punctuality – an importance that is so transparent once a systems view of production is adopted.

This is not to deny that profit-orientated indigenous innovation will occur. It will proceed slowly, however – because, for example, the nature of the innovation may have to be explained with the aid of an expensive foreign-run 'demonstration' plant, as the basic scientific logic cannot be assimilated. Cautious indigenous businessmen may wait for an indigenous innovator to operate successfully before committing themselves. Unfortunately, if the indigenous innovator does not understand the logic of the situation, he may be unable to improvise solutions to unforeseen difficulties, and so the innovation may gain an undeserved reputation for being unworkable.

When significant spillovers do occur, and agglomerations of local industries begin to develop, the effect on the cultural life of the indigenous communities can be devastating. The development of urban areas in which MNE activities are concentrated draws labour away from the rural areas. The migration of rural labour is a selective process. Younger and more entrepreneurial workers are attracted to the towns, leaving the least entrepreneurial workers, and the immigrants' aged dependants, behind. Although rural incomes may be partially sustained by intra-family remittances from the towns, the loss of the more productive and entrepreneurial individuals may well harden the conservative and inward-looking attitudes of those who are left behind. Faced with rising out-migration, the reputation mechanisms that coordinate the activities of rural communities are undermined. Rural economic performance declines, and the dualistic structure of the economy is reinforced.

Meanwhile, cut off from their traditional life-style, new urban workers tend to consume a higher proportion of the convenience products and sophisticated durables marketed by the MNEs. Some of these products are promoted using advertising strongly influenced by Western-style competitive individualism. Instead of creating an urban culture based upon voluntary association, which could lead in the long run to a lively entrepreneurial society, commercial media tend to promote attitudes of unrestrained self-assertion which are inimical both to industrial discipline and to honest business practices.

The social disruption caused by MNE activities does not end here, however. The tradition of subservience to despotic authority, sustained in isolated communities, can sometimes be usefully exploited by MNEs searching for cheap unskilled labour that is easily disciplined by intimidation. Women and children accustomed to absolute paternal authority may become useful factory or plantation employees, for example. Once the women acquire a measure of economic independence, however, the economic basis for paternal authority is undermined, and attempts to sustain it through religious teaching may only be able to slow the trend rather than reverse it. As a result, the whole fabric of traditional family organisation may be thrown into disarray.

Another form of disruption is to encourage mass immigration of refugees or landless peasants from other areas in order to depress wages in the locality of the subsidiary. Besides redistributing income away from labour, this strategy carries major problems of cultural integration within the local community, which may spill over into violence, particularly where the immigrants are readily recognised by their language, style of dress, or physical characteristics.

Finally, there is the political disruption which may result from the fragmentation of political alliances which occurs when some local leaders opt for cooperation with foreign interests whilst others oppose it. Both groups may be forced into extreme positions – one as 'lackeys' of the foreign power and other as intransigent fundamentalists favouring isolation. This fragmentation of the polity may enable the foreign power to 'divide and rule' the country.

This rather negative view of the social consequences of the MNE may be countered by many instances in which MNEs have attempted to become good corporate citizens of the host country. The difficulty here is that many LDCs – particularly former colonies – are in fact agglomerations of different tribes and castes, and that the concept of a good citizen with which the MNE conforms is merely the view held by the social group that is currently in power. Thus in a country with a long history of internal divisions, being officially recognised as a good citizen may require covert discrimination against rival indigenous groups.

Situations of this kind pose various dilemmas for the MNE. In a country, for example, where the religion of the dominant group stresses paternal authority, should contracts for the employment of married women be negotiated through their husbands, so that women in effect become wage-slaves? Is obstructing the economic liberation of women a satisfactory price to pay for being a good corporate citizen and maintaining the economic basis of traditional family life?

In many recently-independent LDCs political power changes frequently, often in response to military initiatives. Should the MNE favour political stability and, if so, use its economic influence on the military to secure the kind of stable regime most acceptable to the liberal Western conscience? If the MNE remains aloof, and instability continues, it is likely to be confronted with a series of corrupt demands for payments to government officials, as the holders of influential offices attempt to make their fortunes before they are deposed in the next change of government. Should the MNE jeopardise the interests, not only of its shareholders, but also of its indigenous employees by refusing to make payments, or should it respect 'local culture' and support the bribery endorsed by the 'unofficial constitution'?

The way managers resolve these moral issues will be determined by the MNE's own corporate culture, which will in turn reflect, at least in part, the national culture of the DC in which it is headquartered. In this respect the balance between the philosophies of competitive individualism and voluntary association in the source country culture will be a critical factor in determining how far broad moral concerns dominate the pursuit of shareholders' short-term interests.

3.9 CONCLUSION

Previous economic literature on MNEs in LDCs has tended to concentrate on issues of market power and the choice of contractual arrangements (for example, Lall and Streeten 1977; Calvet and Naim 1981). The integration of cultural issues into an economic analysis of the subject reflects the authors' belief that economic factors such as these cannot entirely explain the relevant phenomena. This chapter has not proved that cultural factors must be taken into account. It is always possible that some new and more sophisticated economic explanation of these phenomena could be contrived instead. Putting this unlikely possibility to one side, however, this chapter has taken a step towards analysing the way that cultural factors in economic development impact upon, and are modified by, the MNE.

A great deal of further work needs to be done before the hypotheses advanced in this chapter can be properly tested. The full extent of the cultural differences among LDCs, and among the DC countries in which MNEs are based, needs to be recognised. The performance of a given MNE in a given LDC is likely to be governed by (a) the degree of entrepreneurship in the culture of the firm, (b) the degree of entrepreneurship in the culture of the host country, and (c) an 'interaction' or 'coupling' term which captures the overall degree of similarity between the cultures, recognising that culture is a multifaceted phenomenon.

To apply this method it is necessary to profile the cultures of both the entities involved. It may require in-depth interviews with many people to establish profiles which can make any claim to objectivity. Complete objectivity can never be achieved, of course, in any study of cultural phenomena because of the distortion created by the culture-specific prejudices of the observer. Nevertheless, it is unnecessary to go to the other extreme and adopt an entirely relativistic view. Different observers may still be able to agree on some things, even if they cannot agree on everything.

Cultures contain a certain amount of inertia because of the way they are transmitted between generations through family upbringing. Nevertheless, the advent of public education and mass media communications has the potential to accelerate cultural change. The trend towards greater rapidity of cultural change does, indeed, give a sense of urgency to understanding the mechanisms, and the economic effects, involved.

Economic changes can themselves precipitate cultural change, because they affect the shared experiences of members of a society. The increasing interdependence within the world economy is, in fact, another reason why the process of cultural change may have speeded up. This chapter has, unfortunately, treated culture as though it were an exogenous parameter rather than an endogenous variable. A full study of cultural factors would, however, involve a dynamic analysis containing feedback loops of a kind far too complex to be considered here.

Even in its present state, though, the theory provides some simple predictions about comparative economic development. It suggests, for example, that small island economies which enjoy a sophisticated cultural legacy may be better equipped to develop than mainly land-locked countries whose cultural traditions are derived almost exclusively from small isolated rural communities. The entrepôt potential and cultural legacy of Hong Kong, Singapore and Taiwan, say, may therefore explain why they have been able to industrialise and develop indigenous business services so much faster than many sub-Saharan African economies. This is quite consistent with the view that outward-looking trade policies have also promoted their development. It underlines, however, the earlier suggestion that trade policy itself may, in the long run, be culturally specific. Imposing outward-looking trade policies on a less entrepreneurial country in Africa is unlikely to have the same dramatic result as has the voluntary adoption of such policies in South East Asian NICs.

Finally, it should be noted that recognition of cultural factors has significant welfare implications. The emotional benefits that individuals derive from group affiliation are commonly omitted from the preference structures assumed in conventional social cost-benefit analysis of foreign investment. The cultural specificity of the policymaker's own attitudes is also ignored, although these attitudes are crucial in validating the highly materialistic individual preferences assumed in conventional policy analysis. On a more specific level, the failure of conventional analysis to recognise the important economic function of culture in reducing transaction costs, means that conventional analysis has overlooked the significant material as well as emotional costs that cultural disintegration imposes on many sectors of the economy. A number of judgements about the net benefits of foreign investment, derived from conventional analysis, will have to be carefully reconsidered in the light of this cultural analysis.

Acknowledgements

Previous versions of this chapter were given at the EIBA Conference, Antwerp, December 1987, to the Department of Economics seminar at the University of Surrey, October 1988, and to the First Japan AIB Meeting, Waseda University, Tokyo, November 1988. The authors would like to thank the contributors for their comments, and Geoffrey Jones, Matthew McQueen and Hafiz Mirza for comments on an earlier version.

References

Berger, S. and M. J. Piore. 1980. *Dualism and Discontinuity in Industrial Societies* (Cambridge: Cambridge University Press).

Calvet, A. L. and M. Naim. 1981. 'The Multinational Firm in Less Developed Countries: A Markets and Hierarchies Approach', Barcelona, Spain: Paper presented at AIB/EIBA Conference.

Casson, M. C. 1988a. 'The Theory of International Business as a Unified Social Science', University of Reading Discussion Papers in International Investment and Business Studies, Series B, No. 123.

Casson, M. C. 1988b. 'Entrepreneurial Culture as a Competitive Advantage', University of Reading Discussion Papers in International Investment and Business Studies, Series B, No. 124.

Casson, M. C. and R. D. Pearce. 1987. 'Multinational Enterprises in LDCs', in N. Gemmell (ed.), *Surveys in Development Economics* (Oxford: Blackwell), pp. 90–132.

Eisenstadt, S. N. 1973. *Tradition, Change, Modernity* (New York: Wiley).

Hagen, E. E. 1962. *On the Theory of Social Change: How Economic Growth Begins* (Homewood, Illinois: Dorsey Press).

Hayek, F. A. von (1937) 'Economics and Knowledge', *Economica* (New Series), 4, 33–54, reprinted in F. A. von Hayek, *Individualism and Economic Order* (London: Routledge & Kegan Paul, 1949).

Herskovits, M. J. 1961. 'Economic Change and Cultural Dynamics', in R. Braibanti and J. J. Spengler (eds), *Tradition, Values, and Socio-Economic Development* (Durham, NC: Duke University Press), pp. 114–38.

Hirsch, F. 1977. *Social Limits to Growth* (London: Routledge & Kegan Paul).

Hodges, R. 1988. *Primitive and Peasant Markets* (Oxford: Blackwell).

Hoselitz, B. F. 1961. 'Tradition and Economic Growth', in R. Braibanti and J. J. Spengler (eds), *Tradition, Values, and Socio-economic Development* (Durham, NC: Duke University Press), 83–113.

Inkeles, A. and D. H. Smith 1974. *Becoming Modern: Individual Change in Six Developing countries* (London: Heinemann).

Kilby, P. 1971. 'Hunting the Heffalump', in P. Kilby (ed.), *Entrepreneurship and Economic Development* (New York: Free Press), pp. 1–40.

Kirzner, I. M. 1973. *Competition and Entrepreneurship* (Chicago: University of Chicago Press).

Knight, F. H. 1921. *Risk, Uncertainty and Profit*, ed. G. J. Stigler (Chicago: University of Chicago Press).

Lall, S. and P. Streeten. 1977. *Foreign Investment, Transnationals and Developing Countries* (London: Macmillan).

Leff, N. H. 1978. 'Industrial Organisation and Entrepreneurship in the Developing Countries: The Economic Groups', *Economic Development and Cultural Change*, 26, 661–75.

Leibenstein, H. 1978. *General X-efficiency Theory and Economic Development* (New York: Oxford University Press).

McClelland, D. C. and D. G. Winter. 1969. *Motivating Economic Achievement* (New York: Free Press).

Pack, H. 1987. *Productivity, Technology and Economic Development* (New York: Oxford University Press).

Schumpeter, J. A. 1934. *The Theory of Economic Development*, trans. R. Opie (Cambridge, Mass.: Harvard University Press).

Wallerstein, I. 1979. *The Capitalist World-Economy* (Cambridge: Cambridge University Press).

Wiener, M. J. 1981. *English Culture and the Decline of the Industrial Spirit* (Cambridge: Cambridge University Press).

PART II
ORGANISATION

4 Organisational Forms and Multinational Companies

Peter J. Buckley*

4.1 INTRODUCTION

This chapter synthesises several strands of theory which centre on the internal organisation of multinational enterprises. We begin by providing the conceptual framework for this discussion by concentrating on the internalisation approach and the relevance of transaction cost economics for the organisation of multinational firms. After an examination of the literature on the organisation of multinational firms in the light of the transactions cost framework, we then introduce the related, but distinct, internationalisation and globalisation views of the dynamics of the growth of multinational firms. Finally, the interplay of market forces and organisational structure is assessed, and the role of cultural and national influences is analysed, before the various threads in the body of the chapter are drawn together in the conclusion.

4.2 THE INTERNALISATION APPROACH AND TRANSACTION COST ECONOMICS

Several theories of the multinational firm may be identified (Buckley, Chapter 1, in Buckley and Casson 1985; Casson 1986). The ideas of Coase (1937) have been extensively applied to the multinational firm by McManus (1972), Buckley and Casson (1976, 1985), Rugman (1981), and Hennart (1986), in what has become known as the internalisation approach. In addition, Dunning's 'eclectic theory' of the multinational firm (Dunning 1981), combines ownership, internalisation and location-specific advantages in a synthesis of the literature on foreign direct investments. Third,

---

* The author is grateful for comments on a previous draft to Michael Brooke, Richard Butler, Mark Casson and Jean-François Hennart.

Teece (1983) has extended Williamson's (1975) markets and hierarchies approach explicitly to the multinational firm. These approaches attach fundamental importance to the role of transactions costs in the development of multinational firms, and hence distinguish themselves from the work of Hymer (1976) who did not separate market structure problems from those relating to transactions costs.

There has been considerable debate in the literature as to the comparative contributions of these various approaches to the understanding of why firms engage in activities in more than one country. For example, Dunning and Rugman (1985), have examined the extent of Hymer's contribution in terms of the internalisation approach, and Parry (1985) and Rugman (1985) have debated whether internalisation provides a general theory of foreign direct investment. The internalisation and markets and hierarchies approaches have developed their own vocabularies in analysing the multinational firm, but there are close similarities once terminological differences are removed (Williamson 1981, 1985; Casson 1987). However, there are some differences which it is worthwhile highlighting in what follows.

Internalisation

The basic approach of internalisation theorists is marginalist: by carefully specifying the transactional benefits and costs of internalisation which face firms in particular economic circumstances, predictions can be made on the division between internally organised and externally organised markets. A firm will grow by internalising imperfect external markets until it is bounded by markets of which the transactions costs of further internalisation outweigh the transaction cost savings to the firm. The motive for internalisation is profit. Internalisation may be particularly important to gain the benefits of international transfer pricing in order to reduce the firm's overall tax bill, to obtain improved quality control, and to gain vertical integration benefits.[1]

The incidence of transactions costs in internal and external markets can be used to derive propositions on the speed and direction of growth of the firm (Buckley and Casson 1985, Chapter 5; Buckley 1983; Casson 1981).

The purist internalisation view taken by Buckley and Casson (1976, 1985) is that the internal organisation of the multinational firm is an approximation to a perfect market whereby the firm's internal processes are designed to transmit shadow prices to the key decision-makers, which optimise the firm's overall profit. Thus, decentralised profit centres transmit shadow price signals to other decision-makers in cost or profit centres (Buckley 1983). The multinational enterprise is thus a device for reducing transaction costs by buying or creating complementary assets in different nations and integrating their operations within a single unit of control. This is the internal market for intermediate goods and services. In this way, individual managers within the firm have decentralised decision-making powers such that control over the intermediate product actually changes hands as the product moves between plants, although ownership of the product does not (Casson 1981).

Hennart (1986) has drawn parallels between this view and views of economic planning (e.g. Heal 1973). Each decision-maker within the firm maximises his profits, given these internal prices; the firm includes in these prices an optimal tax, leaving members with an income which is just enough to keep them in their present employment (Hennart drawing on Hirschleifer 1956). Thus the approach implies not only a decentralised organisation, but decentralised decision-making based on central determination of goals and distribution of rewards. The organisation necessary to achieve this result is not made explicit, nor does it imply a black and white decentralised or centralised ruling principle. Consequently, an appraisal of the literature with this in mind is timely.

The internalisation approach has strong links with resource dependence approaches to organisational design (see especially Pfeffer and Salancik 1978). The role of management is seen, to a large degree, as reducing or loosening dependencies, deemed as the extent to which the organisation depends upon an external source for a large proportion of its output or input. This is a strong indicator of the direction of growth of a firm towards reducing those dependencies by internalisation of the market in the input (or output) which is crucial to its survival (Buckley and Casson 1976).

Internalisation versus markets and hierarchies

The original objective of the approach adopted by Buckley and Casson (1976) was to use the concept of internalisation of markets to develop a model of the growth of the firm. This has often been abandoned by more recent writers who take technological capability and/or marketing skills and/or management skills as given and, therefore, fixed (Buckley 1983). The most general statement of internalisation is tautologous: firms exist where they minimise transactions costs, and this has led to it being described as 'concept in search of a theory' (Buckley 1983, p. 42). However, it is the wide applicability of internalisation as an explicator of growth which gives the theory its generality, and thus poses dangers. It is therefore necessary to place restrictions on the general theory to give rise to a number of 'special theories' which have empirical content and can be tested (Buckley

1988). By specifying different types of cost which can arise in internal and external markets, these testable proportions can be derived. As a result, it is possible to see a convergence between the internalisation approach and the markets-and-hierarchies approach of Oliver Williamson and others (Williamson 1985, 1975). The markets-and-hierarchies approach to the internal organisation of firms envisages the organisation as a substitute for policing the settlement of disputes: as a privatised (or internalised) legal system. Thus the 'firm as production function needs to make way for the view of the *firm as governance structure* if the ramifications of internal organisation are to be accurately assessed' (Williamson 1981, p. 1539). This notion has been developed by Williamson (1979) and Teece (1983) into 'governance costs' which occur because of incomplete contracting, arising because formal contracts cannot capture tacit knowledge. These problems are resolved by integration of the contractors (internalisation). This enables 'better disclosure, easier agreement, better governance and more efficient transfer' (Teece 1983, p. 55).

The markets-and-hierarchies approach is founded on the twin behavioural assumptions of 'bounded rationality' and 'opportunism'. The former refers to the limited capability of human beings to hold a wide variety of options to complex problem-solving situations. Only a restricted number of options can ever be fully considered and even these cannot be implemented by preparing a completely specified set of contracts in advance. The second recognises that individuals may act in their own interest rather than the organisation's, and this gives rise to potential costs of monitoring and enforcing agreements and contracts (see the Introduction to Francis, Turk and Willman 1983).

These behavioural assumptions – placed in a world where uncertainty and complexity dominate the environment – are subject to the constraint that many assets (including human assets) are specific and difficult to translate across tasks. The constraints of 'asset specificity' are well documented, possibly because this is the simplest concept, in the Williamsonian tool-box, to operationalise. Hierarchy thus becomes the best, though not the only, means of resolving governance costs, given this set of assumptions.

The internalisation approach emphasises an alternative to hierarchy as the means of resolving the problems of monitoring individuals within the organisation and reducing governance costs. Foreign subsidiary managers may have better knowledge of local conditions and thus it may be difficult to use hierarchical direction to remove discretion in decision-making. The same result may be achieved at less cost by altering the incentives to individuals through the imposition of a decentralised shadow pricing system. This involves the managers of subsidiaries (or units within the firm) acting as profit centres and responding to the internal prices set by top managers to achieve the firm's overall objectives (Buckley 1983; Hennart 1986). Hennart suggests that the incentives given by the internal market are more powerful and less costly than hierarchical control, which will only be used when price signals are inappropriate. This has important implications for the centralisation of activities within the multinational firm, as will be seen below.

However, the markets-and-hierarchies and internalisation frameworks are complementary in two important ways: first, they share the view that organisations economise on transactions costs; second, they require the use of supporting assumptions to give empirical content. Much of the empirical content derives from the incidence of transactions costs in internal and external markets. Contributions by Casson (1985), Teece (1983), Buckley (1987), Nicholas (1986) and others have shown that the incidence of transactions costs is particularly high in vertically integrated process industries, knowledge-intensive industries, quality-assurance dependent products and communication-intensive industries. What is crucial is the relative ability of the two approaches to predict *changes* in operational mode (market or firm) – both approaches need to be more fully operationalised (see Teece 1986). But major problems arise in the definition and measurement of transactions costs: the magnitude of transactions costs in relation to transport costs, production costs, marketing and distribution costs must be specified as well as the spatial configuration of their incidence. Causal empiricism suggests that transactions costs are high, but estimates are essential if the theories are to move beyond heuristic models to concrete propositions about market configurations (Buckley 1988). The dynamic considerations must also be drawn out – mirroring an early preoccupation of Williamson (1965).

4.3 THE ORGANISATION OF MULTINATIONAL ENTERPRISES

The previous section has examined the basic tools of analysis of the internalisation approach to multinational enterprises (and to firms in general). This section examines the literature on the organisation of (multinational) firms, tracing its development through the pioneering work of Alfred Chandler and the strategy–structure framework, which attempts to plot the correlation between the objectives of the firm and the internal mechanisms necessary to achieve the firm's goals, to the evolutionary framework of organisational development and the tension between centralising and decentralising pressures. This section ends with a brief examination of principal–agent problems as they apply to the organisation of multinational firms.

The empirical literature on multinational enterprise has developed from the seminal work of Alfred Chandler (1962, 1977) and the ensuing strategy–structure approach. From this, the organisational form of multinationals has been examined in a number of countries and contexts. There is also an intertwined literature on the degree of centralisation in multinationals. This, in turn, is linked with the notion of governance structures. In this discussion, an attempt is made to link these concepts by examining them within the structure introduced in the previous section.

Chandler and the strategy–structure debate

Alfred Chandler's review of the changes in organisation form through multifunction operation to divisionalisation (1962), and the growth and effect of managerial hierarchies (1977), spawned a group of studies of the organisation of multinational firms of different origins: Pavan (1972) on Italy, Rumelt (1974) on the United States, Channon (1973) on the UK, Dyas and Thanheiser (1976) on France and Germany and Wrigley (1978) on Canada. In addition, the painstaking historical work of Mira Wilkins (1970, 1974) on American business abroad has illuminated these processes.

The crude exhortations on organisational design that 'structure should follow strategy' belie the richness of the approach, as a perusal of Chandler's eight basic propositions as to why management (internal) control of economic activity has replaced the market will show (*The Visible Hand* 1977). However, the specification of the relationship between strategy and structure has not always been clear. To some degree, the internalisation framework can help. The direction of growth of the firm, and thus of managerial control, can (to some extent) be predicted if the markets surrounding the firm, and in particular the nature of market imperfections, are understood. Moreover, Chandler's propositions can be given more rigour and predictive content by an injection of the economics of internalisation. Unwise extrapolations of Chandler's analysis can result from excessive attention being given to the firm without adequate consideration of the industrial context in which it is placed and the macroeconomic framework surrounding it.

Organisational forms of multinational enterprises

An immediate distinction must be made, in the analysis of the organisational form of multinationals, between the statutory or legal organisation and the managerial organisation. It is the latter which will be discussed here.

It is conventional to discuss the organisation of multinationals in terms of a framework which is, implicitly at least, evolutionary. The conventional stages approach has suggested an autonomous subsidiary stage, followed by an international division approach, then an international organisational structure and finally a global matrix approach. While such a rigid evolutionary typology is now a thing of the past, the international development of the firm is clearly one major influence on organisational form.

The problems of organising a multinational firm have been considered in the context of various tensions in the firm and external pressures on it. One issue is whether the company should be divided into domestic and international divisions; a second is the direction of managerial line responsibility – should it be subdivided according to major function (marketing, finance, R & D), product lines or geographical area? Arising out of this dilemma is how best to provide for co-ordination with the other two variables, when one of the three key parameters (function, geographical area, product) is chosen as the predominant organisational principle (see *inter alia* Stopford and Wells 1972, Brooke and Remmers 1978).

This literature is equivalent to the M-form debate concerning unitary organisation (U-form) based on product divisions. The work of Chandler (1962, 1977) is usually used as a touchstone. From divisionalisation within a formal administrative structure, traced from the US railroads to the organisational innovations of Pierre S. du Pont and Alfred P. Sloan, the M-form is held to aid (1) strategic planning and (2) monitoring and control of activities through management hierarchies (Williamson 1981). This leads to the view that a global strategy – whereby strategic planning and major policy decisions are taken centrally and implemented worldwide – could only be accomplished through a multi-divisional framework (Stopford and Wells 1972, p. 25). Such an approach remains unnecessarily rigid, and, in an approach allowing greater flexibility, Brooke (1986) interprets an organisation in terms of four main objectives:

(1) enabling decisions to be taken effectively and at the right time,
(2) providing a channel within which to exercise authority,
(3) providing a system for reporting and communication, and
(4) providing a career structure.

Although retaining a basic evolutionary approach, Brooke allows for options at each stage, and for informal pressures as well as formal structures to influence developments. Crucially, he also makes the point that organisational structure at any moment of time is a snapshot of a dynamic process.

Centralisation and decentralisation

The issue of the degree of centralisation of multinational firms has so far been explicitly avoided, even though it is implicitly ever-present. Brooke (1984) sees the organisation as the result, at a point in time, of continuing conflicts to which the firm seeks a resolution. This leads to a dynamic view of organisation structure as an evolving, interim solution. At a moment in time there will be pressures on head office towards greater centralisation and towards greater autonomy for the subsidiary; similarly, these conflicting pressures will operate on the subsidiary (Brooke 1986). Consequently, external pressures will be moderated, directed and influenced by power struggles within the firm. Amongst the most important pressures are, for *centralisation*: (1) the need to direct scarce resources on the basis of worldwide information, (2) the need to pursue the interests of the firm as a whole, even where this conflicts with those of one or more individual subsidiaries (rationalisation is an excellent example), (3) a career structure militating for head office interests; and for *decentralisation*: (1) cost reduction by devolving decision-making, (2) problems of communication, (3) the view that more rapid decision-making results from autonomy, (4) the fact that subsidiary management is more likely to be in tune with local economic conditions, (5) incentive effects arising from freedom in decision-making, (6) external political influences requiring devolved decisions.

The resolution of these pressures depends upon the particular situation of the firm. Of great importance are:

(i)   industry-specific factors such as standardised products, the nature of integration and the nature of the external markets which the firm faces;
(ii) region-specific factors, including the geographical and social distance between the centre and the subsidiaries (these of course influence communication costs)
(iii) nation-specific factors, particularly political and fiscal relations between the countries spanned by the firm;
(iv) factors specific to the firm itself, including the availability of skills and cost of management in each location (these will influence the degree of centralisation) (Buckley and Casson 1976; Brooke 1986).

It is no surprise that the factors which determine the degree of centralisation are also determinants of internalisation, but the two should not be too closely equated. It has been argued, that internalisation is undertaken in order to impose centralisation. For instance, Rugman has argued, 'resource

allocation processes that are internalised are those carried out in a centralised manner' and 'unless R & D is centralised in the parent there is no firm
specific advantage at risk through licensing, yet we know that MNEs prefer
to control the rate of use of their knowledge advantage by direct foreign
investment, thus they must be afraid of dissipation' (Rugman 1981, pp. 29,
105). As pointed out above, it is possible to envisage a situation which
represents the opposite of 'internalisation for centralisation'. By transmit-
ting a set of shadow price signals to decision-makers in subsidiaries acting
as cost or profit centres, the firm operates as closely as possible to a perfect
internal market: this enables the plans of each decision-maker to be meshed
and optimum coordination to be achieved (Buckley 1983).

Principal–agent problems

Whose objectives are paramount in the multinational corporation? Top
decision-makers in the multinational firm face a classic principal–agent
problem. The issue is how best to ensure that managers of foreign subsidiaries respond effectively to the commands or directives of the parent
company. Further, how far are parent company managers responsible to
their principals; the corporate shareholders? This is not the place to review
the literature on ownership and control, but the parent–subsidiary relationship is capable of being analysed as a principal–agent problem. Problems of
monitoring costs (governance costs) loom large in widely-dispersed multinational firms, and the firm, as a network of relationships, must respond to
these demands. It is an outgrowth of the Coasian approach to see the firm
as a set of contractual relationships between individuals (Jensen and Meckling
1976), and a minimisation of costs of contracting and maintaining these
contracts is a driving force of organisational design.

The multinational firm can thus be seen to be analogous to a decentralised socialist economy (following Arrow 1987, pp. 39–40). Knowledge of
(potential) productivity of each (foreign) subsidiary cannot be centralised
and so individual units have information about the possibilities of production
not available to the 'central planning unit'. The subsidiaries may have
incentives not to reveal their full potential because it will be easier to
operate under a less rigorous regime. The problem becomes one of tapping
the subsidiary's information. This is known as incentive compatibility.

Summary

To summarise, this section has analysed a variety of approaches to the
organisation of multinational firms: the strategy–structure view, the organi-

sational form literature, analyses of centralisation and the internal organisation of the firm as a principal–agent problem. A synoptic view, based on the internalisation framework, has been taken. It is clear that there has been a coalescence of views: the feasibility of central management control is a core issue, as is the means by which this control can effectively be exercised; the role of asymmetric information is crucial; both the monitoring and measurement of performance present an underlying difficulty to organisational design; and costs of communication and reward structures have an important role to play. Consequently, there is broad agreement on the key variables which play a role in determining internal organisation. However, the weighting given to the variables differs markedly in the separate approaches. The remainder of this chapter attempts to shed further light on dynamics, the role of market forces and cultural and national factors as they affect organisational structures.

4.4 INTERNATIONALISATION AND GLOBALISATION MODELS OF ORGANISATIONAL CHANGE IN MULTINATIONAL FIRMS

The literature examined in the last section rather begs the questions relating to the process of internationalisation of the firm, its timing and direction. This section examines two parallel, but distinct, models of the development of multinational firms: the 'internationalisation' model, developed largely in Scandinavia and used in European-based studies,[2] and the 'globalisation' model, developed largely in US business schools and used in models of international business strategy.[3]

The internationalisation model, as a generic type, suggests an incremental approach to development: 'deepening involvement' with foreign markets is suggested, a process of 'creeping incrementalism' as the firm grows in international stature. This contrasts with the more grandiose planned globalisation of Porter-type models.

The cautious evolutionary model has been widely applied to small- and medium-sized companies – often those investing abroad for the first time (Buckley, Newbould and Thurwell 1987; Buckley, Berkova and Newbould 1983; Luostarinen 1980). The reaction to risk and uncertainty is a primary determinant of this caution. Firms react to this uncertainty by collecting the appropriate information and learning about foreign conditions by incremental learning and slow organisational development. (Such a process was well described by Aharoni 1966). This information gathering and the 'biased search', applied by Aharoni and others, have a cost implication: the costs of managerial time are a major problem in the planning processes of smaller firms and are an effective constraint on internationalisation and organisational development. The difficulties of recruiting and absorbing an adequate cadre of managers has long been recognised as crucial for organisational change (Penrose 1959).

The applicability and relevance of the internationalisation model must be limited in scope. Young (1987) suggests that it does not apply to 'rapidly changing high technology sectors' (p. 39) because the time scale involved in moving from domestic to foreign manufacture is so short. The phenomenon of shortening product cycles was noted by Giddy (1978) some years ago. Industries with rapid competitor reaction are also an exception, as are industries which are dominated by firms capable of global scanning. It is important to make a distinction between small firms in 'small firm industries' where the average size of firm is low and the representative firm is not widely different from the industry average, where such strategies may be optimal, and small firms in industries dominated by large ones where the long-run future of smaller competitors is bleak. Firms practising 'niche strategies' may be able to pursue caution, but the increasing pace of change in many industries may render this strategy less than widely applicable.

However, the same issue arises with the globalisation thesis[4] – what is the industrial range of its application? In its pure form – the implication of a global product, standardised marketing techniques and centralised planning and control – the answer is that probably not many sectors, industries or product divisions conform to a homogeneous worldwide strategy. Perhaps the model is an idealised view of the organisation of firms at the opposite end of the size spectrum from the internationally naive first-time foreign investors? National markets in many areas remain firmly idiosyncratic. The focus of most analysts on successful multinationals leads us to ignore the many failed attempts to impose a foreign (international or global) product on an unwilling national market. Moreover, the existence of market niches leaves global marketeers vulnerable to competitors from non-standardised products.

Consequently, a more cautious version of the globalisation model is now the norm. Porter's recent work (1986) suggests that there is not a single global strategy (Young 1987): rather, a strategy is constrained by the value chain (i.e. vertical integration imperatives), configuration (location costs of interrelated activities internalised within the firm) and coordination issues. This leads to a typology of global strategies. A related categorisation by White and Poynter (1984) distinguishes the types of integration amongst networks of foreign affiliates (miniature replica, marketing satellites, rationalised manufacture, product specialist and strategic independent). This has much in common with Casson's typology arising from a recent study of multinationals and world trade which relies on an extended version of the product cycle to analyse changes in the international division of labour. Casson provides a typology of industries: new product industries, mature product industries, rationalised product industries, resource-based industries and trading and non-tradeable service industries in which intra-firm trade (and therefore the organisation of the firm) can be studied (Casson 1986).

Consequently, from a rather disparate literature on the international development of the firm, several key points can be distilled. First, both the size of the firm and its history influence organisation. Second, the nature of the industry and its relationship to, and influence on, individual firms is of great importance. Third, a complex interaction between changes in the international division of labour (through intra-firm trade to organisational development) is at work, and these elements must be studied in an interactive framework to enable a full comprehension of the processes at work. The following section analyses the interaction between firm and market in order to elucidate these issues.

4.5 MARKET FORCES AND ORGANISATIONAL STRUCTURE

How far are organisational structures under the control of management? How much of organisational design is actually determined by external market pressures? Economists, including those advocating internalisation as a major influence on the growth of firms, see the market as paramount. Organisational theorists and management writers often appear to believe that management can decide upon and impose not only a strategy but also a structure on the world economy. Clearly there is an interaction: the greater the degree of market power, the greater the degree of management discretion. The contestability of markets will be a major constraint on organisational form.

Many writers view organisations in an implicitly social Darwinist framework. Those which fail to achieve survival levels of profit will be killed off either by failure (bankruptcy) or absorption of predators (takeovers). Whilst there is no doubt that the pressures of the market and of the takeover threat constrain organisations towards efficient organisational modes, the degree of observed organisational diversity suggests that inertia is strong in many areas.

Part of this diversity is perhaps explicable by reference to the 'dualism' in the nature of the multinational firm, pointed out initially by Hymer (1976): one element is the market power possessed by most large multinational firms, typically operating in an oligopolistic world market; the

second is the multinational firm's transaction costs minimising role emphasised in internalisation approaches. Whilst market power, or the possession
of firm specific advantages is not a defining characteristic of multinational
firms, nor a necessary condition for their existence (Casson 1986), there is
no doubt that market power is often associated with large multinationals.
Again, the importance of linking the firm to the industry is apparent in the
analysis of organisation. The existence of organisational slack or X-
inefficiency is directly linked to non-competitive situations. Attempts to
extend market power by takeovers of competitors, joint ventures, implicit or
explicit cartels and the response to antitrust or anti-monopoly legislation
obviously further influence organisational form.

A third principle

The distinction between firm and market as major principles of organisation
is analytically precise but has been challenged as inadequate. The role of
cooperation between firms can be traced back to G. B. Richardson's 1972
article 'The Organisation of Industry' which points to a 'dense network of
cooperation and affiliation by which firms are interrelated' (p. 833).[5]
Subcontracting, supplier relationships in manufacturing and marketing and
the pooling or transfer of technology are given as examples of planned
coordination across firm boundaries. This 'third principle' of organisation
has been seized upon by Kojima and Ozawa (1984b) to explain the group
investment activities of Sogo Shosha (Japanese general trading companies).
    Parallel to Richardson's discovery, a paper by Brown (1984) shows that,
as well as the widely acknowledged market-like behaviour in firms, there
also exists firm-like behaviour in markets through administered marketing
channels arising from non-pecuniary influences of one channel partner on
another.
    A further development is the work of Imai and Itami (1984) who dis-
tinguish 'area' and 'principle' in resource allocation mechanisms. They
divide the competing principles of allocation (1) by the type of decision-
making transaction, and (2) by membership of participants and their mutual
relationships ('arena') to arrive at a classification of resource allocation
mechanisms (see Figure 4.1). They then compare US allocation systems
with Japanese systems, finding that their conceptualisation explains stylised
differences between the two economies.
    A further attempt to integrate cooperative ventures into the theory has
been made by Buckley and Casson (1987) as 'coordination effected through
mutual forbearance', identifying cooperation as a special type of coordination.
They analyse the conditions under which cooperation leads to an increase in

Decision-making principal \ Membership of participants and their mutual relationship 'Arena'	M_2	$M_2 + O_2$	O_2
M_1	Pure market	Organisation-like market	
$M_1 + O_1$	Organisation-like market	Intermediate organisation	Market-like organisation
O_1		Market-like organisation	Pure organisation

Source: After Imai and Itami (1984) especially p. 289.

Notes: $M_1 =$ free private interest maximisation in which price, or some other equivalent signal, is used as a major medium of information
$M_2 =$ free entry and exit
$O_1 =$ direction based on authority, for common interest maximisation
$O_2 =$ fixed and continual relationship

FIGURE 4.1   *Interpenetration of organisation and market*

efficiency, and they define the meaning of forbearance.

Forbearance arises when one party refrains from cheating another party. Transactions-cost economics recognises that all parties in a venture have a potential for self-interested opportunism. Thus aggression can arise when one party perpetrates an act which damages another party's interests; a weaker form of cheating is to refrain from an act which would benefit someone else – this is termed neutrality. Consequently, actions can be classified as: taking advantage of another party (strong cheating), refraining from either taking advantage of them or helping them (weak cheating) or assisting them (forbearance). Forbearance is a useful concept in the analysis of the negotiations leading up to a joint venture and its continuation. The analysis is confined to the single, but crucial, case of 50:50 joint ventures between independent firms. Joint ventures are explained in terms of a combination of economies of internalisation, indivisibilities and obstacles to merger. It is possible to analyse joint ventures using conventional economic analysis because they are shown to compromise contractual arrangements which minimise transactions costs under certain environmental constraints. However, the analysis contains not only the concept of forbearance but also those of trust, reputation and commitment – concepts not normally encountered in economic analysis. Joint ventures are found to be, in certain circumstances, devices by which the parties can demonstrate mutual forbearance and thus build up trust; and trust is shown to be both an input and an output of joint ventures. Dynamic considerations can be built in by the analysis of reputation effects, which are the result of repeated instances of forbearance. However, it is also the case that joint ventures are often devices for enhancing collusion and for luring 'partners' into unfavourable deals. Development of this type of analysis would seem to promise benefits in the understanding of organisational problems.

This analysis brings in an element of altruism – or, at least, the sacrifice of short-term opportunistic gains for longer-term aims – which the Williamson framework lacks (Francis, Turk and Willman 1983, p. 6). It may well prove fruitful, for instance, in the analysis of Japanese multinationals for precisely this reason. However, Williamson acknowledges the importance of 'both institutional and personal trust relations' (Williamson and Ouchi 1983, p. 19). In outlining the future research agenda of the markets and hierarchies programme, further emphasis is placed on the frequency and uncertainty of transactions, which accords well with the evolving dynamic elements of the internalisation programme (Buckley 1983) as well as transaction-specific investment (Williamson and Ouchi 1983, p. 33).

The importance of influences which are not conventionally 'market' or 'firm' (neither are they easily resolved into these two components) is thus acknowledged in the literature. In examining the detailed issues of the allocation of resources and rights, a simple dichotomy – firm and market – often will not convey the richness of organisational design. However, it is important not to forget that the purpose of a theory is to explain as wide a variety of observed phenomena as possible with a parsimonious set of axioms, otherwise, there is a danger that theory will slip into simple description or an arid taxonomy. In order to be explanatory and predictive, the analysis must explain the mechanism by which one organisational principle changes into another, and the conditions which precipitate that change. The incidence of the costs and benefits of the cooperative firm must be specified as well as the shift from firm to market, and vice versa, otherwise its introduction allows the analysis to decline into description. In other words, Richardson's framework requires further operationalising in the way that

Coase's 1937 article has been operationalised by Buckley and Casson (1976) and others.

4.6 CULTURAL AND NATIONAL INFLUENCES ON ORGANISATIONAL FORM

It is undeniable that national and cultural differences influence the organisation of multinational firms originating from different backgrounds. A review of the empirical literature suggests that the multi-divisional form (M-form) of organisation has developed at different rates in different countries – more specifically, less in Japan than in the USA, Britain and West Germany (Steer and Cable 1978, Cable and Dirrheimer 1983, Cable and Yasuki 1985). Japan's relative slowness in adopting the M-form organisation may be attributed to the macro-environment; most notably the membership of business groups by Japanese firms. Pinpointing the similarities and differences in firms of different nationalities is the stock-in-trade of cross-cultural studies. The imperatives of international competition notwithstanding, strong differences arising from country of origin still persist. As an example, the market-servicing strategies of firms of different nationalities persist within the same industry, even after allowing for the effects of size (Buckley and Pearce 1979, 1981, 1984).

One important influence is that of domestic economic structure (Buckley 1985) – an obvious example of this is the imperative of resource-poor nations to spawn multinationals in order to control key (foreign-located) inputs. Other aspects likely to affect the organisation of multinational firms include: the significant influence of home government policies on multinationals' control regulation or encouragement; the influence of the parent company's configuration on the form of outward investment; the attraction of offshore production (designed to benefit from low-cost labour) when domestic labour is expensive or troublesome; and the appeal of tax havens to multinationals from high tax countries.

In the case of radically different organisational forms, such as the general trading companies of Japan (Sogo Shosha), it has been suggested that a different explanation from the internalisation approach is required (Kojima 1973, 1978, 1982; Kojima and Ozawa 1984a, 1948b, 1985). The use of specific information in a confidential manner within Sogo Shosha has a direct parallel with the development of international merchant banks in other advanced economies. The relatively underdeveloped nature of the pure capital market in Japan is a major reason for this development. Thus, the use of internal capital markets within Sogo Shosha is a response to the institutions of the home country.

In contrast, such services in the UK and USA have developed within specialised banks operating in the external market for capital. As Yannopoulos (1983) has pointed out, there are differences among countries in the availability of information inputs characterised by high communication costs; the performance of services requiring these inputs necessitates a local physical presence. These facts contain the explanatory 'germ' of the development of transnational banks and the international expansion of Sogo Shosha.

4.7 CONCLUSION

It is immediately apparent that many of the issues, problems and conceptual difficulties in the analysis of the organisational form of multinational enterprises are common to the analysis of any organisation. This should not be a surprise. The multinational firm is a special case of commercial organisation – a polar extreme, not a different category. However, it holds more interest for the organisational specialist because it encompasses cultural, national and regional differences.

This chapter has shown that a coherent framework for the analysis of the organisation of multinationals as a generic type does exist: the use of internalisation framework gives a set of central concepts with great analytical power. The scope of the firm has, until recently, been the main dependent variable which the framework has been used to explain rather than its organisation. However, in drawing together literature on the organisation of multinational firms – on strategy and structure, centralisation and decentralisation, internationalisation and globalisation, market and firm and the role of cultural and national differences – the internalisation approach provides a bonding element which is capable of leading to synthesis.

It is essential to realise that any synthesis of literature on the organisation of multinationals must cope with dynamics. As international competition evolves so too does organisational design. Multinationals are adaptive and innovative organisations whose very competitive strength depends upon response to changing environments. Any modelling which assumes a static framework is doomed. Consequently, a successful analysis must be able to deal with change. In this respect, the underlying framework given here must commend itself for its simplicity and predictive power.

Notes

1. The benefits of international internalisation frequently arise from the opportu-
    nities to reduce the firm's overall tax liability. As much government interven-
    tion depends on (amongst other things) the valuation of traded intermediate
    goods, internal markets provide an ideal opportunity to reduce tax liabilities
    and other forms of government intervention. Imputed prices of intermediate
    goods in internal markets can include a tax limiting factor, particularly in
    markets for knowledge (or knowledge-intensive goods), the valuation of which
    is notoriously difficult. Multinational firms may impute mark-ups in the
    lowest tax countries and may alter their location strategy in order to include a
    low intervention 'tax haven'. Evidence on transfer pricing is provided in Lall
    (1973, 1978) and Rugman and Eden (1985) and a classificatory scheme is
    given by Plasschaert (1981). Evidence on the nature and amount of intra-
    company trade is given by Buckley and Pearce (1979, 1981, 1984).
2. A selection of references is: Carlson (1975), Johanson and Vahlne (1977),
    Luostarinen (1978), Welch and Wiedersheim-Paul (1980, a, b), Wiedersheim-
    Paul (1972), Cavusgil (1972), Juul and Walters (1987).
3. References are available in Porter (1986b).
4. Models of globalisation owe a great deal in conception to the earlier genera-
    tion of product cycle models deriving from Vernon's (1966) path-breaking
    article.
5. See also Thompson (1967).

References

Aharoni, Yair. 1966. *The Foreign Investment Decision Process* (Boston, Mass.,
    Graduate School of Business Administration, Harvard University).
Arrow, Kenneth J. 1987. 'The Economics of Agency' in John W. Pratt and Richard
    J. Zeckhauser (eds), *Principals and Agents: The Structure of Business* (Boston,
    Mass., Harvard Business School Press).
Brooke, Michael Z. 1984. *Centralization and Autonomy* (Eastbourne: Holt, Rinehart
    and Winston).
Brooke, Michael Z. 1986. *International Management: A Review of Strategies and
    Operations* (London: Hutchinson).
Brooke, Michael Z. and Remmers, H. Lee. 1978. *The Strategy of Multinational
    Enterprise*, 2nd ed. (London: Pitman).
Brown, Wilson B. 1984. 'Firm Like Behaviour in Markets – The Administered
    Channel', *International Journal of Industrial Organisation*, Vol. 2, pp. 263–76.
Buckley, Peter J. 1983. 'New Theories of International Business: Some Unresolved
    Problems' in Mark Casson (ed.), *The Growth of International Business* (London:
    George Allen & Unwin).
Buckley, Peter J. 1985. 'The Economic Analysis of the Multinational Enterprise:
    Reading versus Japan?', *Hitotsubashi Journal of Economics*, Vol. 26, no. 2,
    December, pp. 117–24.
Buckley, Peter J. 1986. 'The Limits of Explanation – Tests of the Theory of
    Multinational Enterprise', Academy of International Business Annual Meeting,
    London.

Buckley, Peter J. 1987. 'An Economic Transactions Analysis of Tourism' *Tourism Management*, Vol. 87, no. 3, September, pp. 190–94.

Buckley, Peter J. 1988. 'The limits of explanation: Testing the internationalisation theory of the multinational enterprise', *Journal of International Business Studies*, Summer, 2: 181–93.

Buckley, Peter J., Berkova, Zdenka and Newbould, Gerald D. 1983. *Direct Investment in the UK by Smaller European Firms* (London: Macmillan).

Buckley, Peter J. and Casson, Mark. 1976. *The Future of the Multinational Enterprise* (London: Macmillan).

Buckley, Peter J. and Casson, Mark. 1985. *The Economic Theory of the Multinational Enterprise: Selected Readings.* (London: Macmillan).

Buckley, Peter J. and Casson, Mark. 1987. 'A Theory of Cooperation in International Business', in *Cooperative Strategies in International Business*, ed. by F J Contractor and P Lorange (Lexington Books, D C Heath and Co.). Also in *Management International Review* 1987.

Buckley, Peter J., Newbould, Gerald D. and Thurwell, Jane. 1987. *Foreign Direct Investment by Smaller UK Firms.* (London: Macmillan). First edition published as *Going International – The Experiences of UK Firms Overseas.* (London: Associated Business Press, 1978).

Buckley, Peter J. and Pearce, Robert D. 1979. 'Overseas Production and Exporting by the World's Largest Enterprises – A Study in Sourcing Policy', *Journal of International Business Studies*, 10.1, pp. 9–20.

Buckley, Peter J. and Pearce, Robert D. 1981. 'Market Servicing by Multinational Manufacturing Firms: Exporting versus Foreign Production', *Managerial and Decision Economics*, 2.4, pp. 229–46.

Buckley, Peter J. and Pearce, Robert D. 1984. 'Exports in the Strategy of Multinational Enterprises', *Journal of Business Research* 12.2, pp. 209:226.

Cable, John and Dirrheimer, Manfred F. 1983. 'Hierarchies and Markets: An Empirical Test of the Multidivisional Hypothesis in West Germany', *International Journal of Industrial Organisation*, 1, pp. 43–62.

Cable, John and Yasuki, Hirohiko. 1985. 'Internal Organisation, Business Groups and Corporate Performance: An Empirical Test of the Multidivisional Hypothesis in Japan', *International Journal of Industrial Organisation*, 3, pp. 401–20.

Carlson, Sune. 1975. *How Foreign Is Foreign Trade?* (Uppsala: University of Uppsala).

Casson, Mark. 1981. 'Foreword' to Alan M. Rugman, *Inside the Multinationals* (London: Croom Helm).

Casson, Mark. 1985. 'Transaction Costs and the Theory of the Multinational Enterprise' in Buckley and Casson 1985, op. cit.

Casson, Mark (ed.). 1986. *Multinationals and World Trade* (London: George Allen & Unwin).

Casson, Mark, 1987. *The Firm and the Market* (Oxford: Basil Blackwell).

Cavusgil, S. Tamer. 1972. 'Some Observations on the Relevance of Critical Variables for Internationalisation Stages', *Export Management*, ed. by M. R. Czinkota and G. Tesar (New York: Praeger).

Chandler, Alfred D., Jr. 1962. *Strategy and Structure: Chapters in the History of the Industrial Enterprise* (Cambridge, Mass.: MIT Press).

Chandler, Alfred D., Jr. 1977. *The Visible Hand: The Managerial Revolution in American Business* (Cambridge, Mass.: Belknap Press).

80 *Studies in International Business*

Channon, Derek F. 1973. *The Strategy and Structure of British Enterprise* Division of Research, Graduate School of Business Administration, Harvard University, Boston, Mass.

Coase, Ronald H. 1937. 'The Nature of the Firm', *Economica* (New Series) Vol. 4, pp. 386–405.

Dunning, John H. 1981. *International Production and the Multinational Enterprise* (London: George Allen & Unwin).

Dyas, Gareth P. and Thanheiser, Heinz T. (1976) *The Emerging European Enterprise: Strategy and Structure in French and German Industry*, (London: Macmillan).

Francis, Arthur, Turk, Jeremy and Willman, Paul (eds). 1983. *Power, Efficiency and Institutions* (London: Heinemann).

Giddy, Ian H. 1978. 'The Demise of the Product Cycle in International Business Theory', *Columbia Journal of World Business*, 13.1, pp. 90–7.

Heal, Geoffrey M. 1973. *The Theory of Economic Planning*. (Amsterdam: North-Holland).

Hennart, Jean-François. 1986. 'What is Internalisation?' *Weltwirtschaftliches Archiv*, 122, 4, pp. 791–804.

Hirshleifer, Jack. 1956. 'On the Economics of Transfer Pricing', *The Journal of Business*, Vol. 29, pp. 172–84.

Hymer, Stephen H. 1976. *The International Operations of National Firms* (Lexington, Mass.: Lexington Books).

Imai, Ken-ichi and Itami, Hiroyuki. 1984. 'Interpenetration of Organisation and Market', *International Journal of Industrial Organization*, 161, 2, pp. 285–310.

Jensen, Michael C. and Meckling, William H. 1976. 'Theory of the Firm: Managerial Behaviour Agency Costs and Ownership Structure', *Journal of Financial Economics*, Vol. 3, pp. 305–60.

Johanson, Jan and Vahlne, Jan Erik. 1977. 'The Internationalisation Process of the Firm – A Model of Knowledge Development and Increasing Foreign Market Commitments', *Journal of International Business Studies*, 8.1, pp. 23–32.

Juul, M. and Walters, P. G. P. 1987. The Internationalisation of Norwegian firms – A Study of the UK Experience, *Management International Review*. 27.1, pp. 58–66.

Kojima, Kiyoshi. 1973. 'A Macroeconomic Approach to Foreign Direct Investment', *Hitotsubashi Journal of Economics*, Vol. 23, pp. 1–19.

Kojima, Kiyoshi. 1978. *Direct Foreign Investment*, (Beckenham: Croom Helm).

Kojima, Kiyoshi. 1982. 'Macroeconomic versus International Business Approach to Direct Foreign Investment', *Hitotsubashi Journal of Economics*, Vol. 25, pp. 1–20.

Kojima, Kiyoshi and Ozawa, Terutomo. 1984a. 'Micro and Macro Economic Models of Direct Foreign Investment', *Hitotsubashi Journal of Economics*, Vol. 25, pp. 1–20.

Kojima, Kiyoshi and Ozawa, Terutomo. 1984b. *Japan's General Trading Companies: Merchants of Economics Development* (Paris: OECD).

Kojima, Kiyoshi and Ozawa. 1985. 'Towards a Theory of Industrial Restructuring and Dynamic Comparative Advantage', *Hitotsubashi Journal of Economics*, Vol. 26, pp. 135–45.

Luostarinen, Reijo. 1978. 'Internationalization Process of the Firm', Working Papers in International Business 1978/1, Helsinki School of Economics.

Luostarinen, Reijo. 1980. *Internationalization of the Firm* (Helsinki: Helsinki School of Economics).

Nicholas, Stephen J. 1986. 'Multinationals, Transaction Costs and Choice of Institutional Form', University of Reading Discussion Papers in International Investment and Business Studies, No. 97.

Pavan, Robert J. 1972. *The Strategy and Structure of Italian Enterprise*, unpublished DBA thesis, Graduate School of Business Administration, Harvard University.

Penrose, Edith T. 1959. *The Theory of the Growth of the Firm*. (Oxford: Basil Blackwell).

Pfeffer, Jeffrey and Salancik, Gerald R. 1978. *The External Control of Organisations: A Resource Dependence Perspective* (New York: Harper & Row).

Porter, Michael E. (ed.). 1986. *Competition in Global Industries* (Boston, Mass.: Harvard Business School Press).

Richardson, G. B. 1972. 'The Organisation of Industry', *Economic Journal*, Vol. 82, pp. 883–96.

Rugman, Alan M. 1981. *Inside the Multinationals* (London: Croom Helm).

Rumelt, Richard P. 1974. *Strategy, Structure and Economic Performance*. Division of Research, Graduate School of Business Administration, Harvard University, Boston, Mass.

Steer, Peter and Cable, John. 1978. 'Internal Organization and Profit: An Empirical Analysis of Large UK Companies', *Journal of Industrial Economics*. Vol. XXVII, No. 1, September, pp. 13–30.

Stopford, John M. and Wells, Louis T., Jr. 1972. *Managing the Multinational Enterprise: Organization of the Firm and Ownership of the Subsidiaries* (London: Longman).

Teece, David T. 1983. 'Technological and Organisational Factors in the Theory of the Multinational Enterprise' in Mark Casson (ed.), *The Growth of International Business* (London: George Allen & Unwin).

Teece, David J. 1986. 'Transaction Cost Economics and the Multinational Enterprise: An Assessment', *Journal of Economic Behaviour and Organisation*, 7, pp. 21–45.

Vernon, Raymond. 1966. 'International Investment and International Trade in the Product Cycle', *Quarterly Journal of Economics*. Vol. 80, pp. 190–207.

Welch, Laurence and Wiedersheim-Paul, Finn. 1980a. 'Domestic Expansion – Internationalization at Home', *South Carolina Essays in International Business*, 2.

Welch, Laurence and Wiedersheim-Paul, Finn. 1980b. 'Initial Exports – A Marketing Failure', *Journal of Management Studies*, 17.3.

White, R. G. and Poynter, T. A. 1984. Strategies for Foreign-Owned Subsidiaries in Canada, *Business Quarterly*.

Wiedersheim-Paul, Finn. 1972. *Uncertainty and Economic Distance* Uppsala Studies in International Business, Uppsala University.

Wilkins, Mira. 1970. *The Emergence of Multinational Enterprise: American Business Abroad from the Colonial Era to 1914*. (Cambridge, Mass.: Harvard University Press).

Wilkins, Mira. 1974. *The Maturing of Multinational Enterprise: American Business Abroad from 1914 to 1970*. (Cambridge, Mass.: Harvard University Press).

Williamson, Oliver E. 1964. 'A Dynamic Theory of Interfirm Behaviour', *Quarterly*

Journal of Economics, Vol. LXXIX, no. 4, November, pp. 579–607.

Williamson, Oliver E. 1975. *Markets and Hierarchies: Analysis and Anti-Trust Implications* (New York: Free Press).

Williamson, Oliver E. 1979. 'Transaction Cost Economics: The Governance of Contractual Relations', *Journal of Law and Economics*, Vol. 22, no. 2.

Williamson, Oliver E. 1981. 'The Modern Corporation: Origins, Evaluation, Attributes', *Journal of Economic Literature*, Vol. XIX, pp. 1537–68.

Williamson, Oliver E. 1985. *The Economic Institutions of Capitalism: Firms, Markets, Relational Contracting* (New York: Free Press).

Williamson, Oliver E. and Ouchi, W. G. 1983. 'The Markets and Hierarchies Programme of Research: origins, implications, prospects', in Arthur Francis, Jeremy Turk and Paul Willman (eds), op cit.

Wrigley, Leonard. 1978. 'Conglomerate Growth in Canada', School of Business Administration, University of Western Ontario, mimeo.

Yannopoulos, George N. 1983. 'The Growth of Transnational Banking' in Mark Casson (ed.) *The Growth of International Business* (London: George Allen & Unwin).

Young, Stephen. (1987). 'Business Strategy and the Internationalization of Business: Recent Approaches', *Managerial and Decision Economics*, 8.1, pp. 31–40.

5 The Institutionalist Perspective on Recent Theories of Direct Foreign Investment: A Comment on McClintock

Peter J. Buckley

If Brent McClintock is right in his view that institutional analysts are to become more involved in the debate on the analysis of direct foreign investment and the multinational enterprise, then this is much to be welcomed (McClintock 1988). However, in undertaking such an analysis, prospective institutional analysts of the multinational enterprise should take care not to reinvent the wheel. They should also be aware of the many points of contact that exist within existing theorising for the inclusion of greater institutional analysis. As one named by McClintock as 'a practitioner' of the internalisation approach, I will accept that label and suggest that this approach represents the most suitable type of analysis to benefit from greater institutionalist inputs (McClintock 1988, p. 478).

The original attempt by Buckley and Mark Casson to fuse the neoclassical analysis of the firm with institutional elements may now be seen as conceding too much to the neoclassical position (Buckley and Casson 1989). Attempts to refine the theory have been made by the original proponents (Buckley and Casson 1985; Casson 1987; Buckley 1988) and others, but there are several more promising avenues still to be followed. These include: (1) the infusion of more radical (to neoclassical economists) elements such as forbearance, trust, reciprocity, commitment in an overarching concept of cooperation, particularly in the context of joint ventures (Buckley and Casson 1988), (2) the inclusion of corporate culture more specifically within the analysis, and (3) more explicit attention to the welfare implications of multinationals.

NEW CONCEPTS IN THE ANALYSIS OF THE MULTINATIONAL ENTERPRISE

It has been apparent for some time that the multinational enterprise as an institution has been changing its nature. The old concept of a centrally controlled, hierarchical, monolithic firm that engages in foreign business only through wholly-owned foreign subsidiaries cannot be upheld as a true description of the multinational firm in the world economy of the late 1980s. The advent of new forms of international involvement (or more accurately their recognition) is a graphic illustration of the adaptability of the multinational firm. The use of licensing in its many forms, joint ventures, minority holdings, fade-out agreements, management contracts, turnkey ventures and international subcontracting are all examples of modes of cooperation with external entities (Buckley 1985a). These new forms require an analysis that transcends the firm, considers alternative modes of doing business abroad and yet remains analytical rather than merely descriptive.

The joint venture represents an excellent test case of the operational effectiveness of theories of the multinational enterprise. More particularly, the special case of the 50:50 joint venture, where control is truly shared, may be taken as an illustration of a genuinely cooperative organisation.

The analysis undertaken by Buckley and Casson (1988) attempts to pinpoint the extent to which ostensibly cooperative ventures are in practice genuinely so, and to define rigorously the concept of cooperation. Cooperation is defined as 'coordination effected through mutual forbearance' (Buckley and Casson 1988, p. 32). Forbearance is the action of giving up opportunities for short-term gain at another party's expense in the hope of achieving reciprocal behaviour on that party's behalf so that it achieves a more optimal long-run outcome than could be achieved by antagonistic behaviour.

Theoretical underpinning from another area is provided by R. Axelrod (1984). Parties who refrain from cheating in agreements (that is, those who forbear), gain a reputation that enables potential partners to identify likely successful cooperation. Thus a reputation is an investment. Inputs of cooperation enhance the reputation, which leads to greater outputs of cooperation. This build-up of mutual trust can take the cooperation into a further phase where, rather than pursuing the cooperative venture for strategic reasons, the parties became committed to cooperative behaviour for its own sake. This latter argument takes the analysis beyond the bounds of the neoclassical approach, for it amounts to a postulate that the agent's preferences cease to depend on material profit alone but are also characteristic of the ventures in which the agent is involved; surely an institutionalist position!

Corporate cultures

The inclusion of the impact of corporate culture in the analysis of the multinational firms is an urgent task, but it has already begun. A transactions cost analysis of the multinational firm enables us to see that it is possible to achieve functional separation in the international capital market so that funding (postponing consumption so that an asset can be produced) can be performed by nationals of one country, ownership (and its associated risk-bearing), by a second group of nationals, and utilisation (with its associated form of risk), by a third group (Cassson 1985a). Utilizers may be identified largely with managers. Consequently, managers of one national group may be operating assets under the ownship of those from another nationality who are funded from elsewhere. In this potentially complex pattern, the role of culture must be specified carefully. There has been, for instance, an unfortunate tendency for many writers to exaggerate the differences between, for example, Japan and 'the West' (for a critique see Buckley and Mirza 1985). The 'uniqueness' of any (national) culture is open to question. Most countries and ownership groups of firms share common traditions with their neighbours. Shared values are also attributed to groups of nations that have shown either spectacular growth (the newly industrialising countries (NICs)) or stagnation. What requires explanation, however, are shifts in growth and development patterns – such as the rapid growth and industrialisation of Japan and the NICs. Culture is a very poor means of explaining such shifts. The *same* factor (Confucianism, Islam, et cetera) cannot be adduced as a contributing factor to stagnation and then as a growth promoter, unless significant and simultaneous changes in culture can be shown. If this can be shown, then culture is endogenous, not exogenous.

There is, however, one particular area where a culture-based hypothesis may contribute to the internalisation approach. It may be plausible to suggest that some cultures are more conducive to the attributes needed to manage internal markets than are others. It may be suggested that cultures that emphasise group solidarity, cooperation, and shared rewards may prove superior in managing internal markets (which may be an analogue of management itself!). Even this hypothesis requires careful handing. A further element in the theory of the multinational enterprise is the role of entrepreneurship (Casson 1985b; Buckley 1988). It is often suggested that the values underlying entrepreneurial flair are antithetical to those requiring sound management of an internal market. Thus, self-reliance, individualism, concern for material reward and risk-taking are emphasised as the cultural underpinnings of entrepreneurship. Cultural explanations of the growth of the multinational enterprise thus have a long way to go before any definitive hypotheses can be added to the existing explanation. There is much work for institutionalists to do!.

Welfare implications

McClintock's rather partial reading of the internalisation approach leads him to believe that the Kojima/Ozawa view on welfare implications of the multinational enterprise 'is perhaps the most even handed' (McClintock 1988, p. 481). Elsewhere, I have tried to rebut this proposition (Buckley 1985b). However, the internalisation approach does recognise both welfare gains and welfare losses arising from the establishment and growth of the multinational firm. Welfare gains arise where the replacement of an imperfect external market results in the internal market being a superior allocator or when 'market making' activities result in an internal market where none existed before: 'internalisation of an externality'. Welfare losses arise where multinationals maximise monopoly profits by restricting the output of goods and services and where vertical integration is used as an entry barrier. Further, multinationals may reduce social efficiency because they provide a more suitable mechanism for exploiting an international monopoly than does a cartel – that is, by internalising collusive agreements, multinationals make the enforcement of collusion more effective (Buckley and Casson 1985). Thus the *static* welfare implications represent a tension between 'asset power' (Teece 1983) and transaction cost economies brought about by internalisation.

Much more important are the dynamic elements in the internalisation approach. The internal market allows greater interplant and functional cooperation (as between production, marketing and research and development). In the long run, this will stimulate both the undertaking of innovation and its effective implementation in the output of new goods and services, improved product quality and lower prices. Consequently, there will be a dynamic improvement in welfare. This argument has much in common with the approach pioneered by Joseph Schumpeter (1934).

THE INSTITUTIONALIST PERSPECTIVE ON THE MULTINATIONAL ENTERPRISE

McClintock suggests four main areas where institutionalists may contribute to the study of the multinational enterprise: the cultural motivations involved in cross-national operation, the theory of the multinational enterprise, international governance, and instrumental value theory. The first two were covered above.

McClintock underestimates the extent to which international governance has been treated in the literature on multinational enterprises. This issue has been treated in the literature from at least the time of Stephen P. Hymer's thesis and C. P. Kindleberger's expansion of it (Hymer 1969; Kindleberger 1969). Raymond Vernon has been particularly concerned with this issue over the years and has treated the issue extensively (Vernon 1971; 1977). The issues of international governance are now examined extensively in international business texts (see for example, Alan M. Rugman, Donald J. Lecraw, and Laurence D. Booth [1985]; see also John Robinson [1983]).

Given the neoclassical framework from which the theory of multinational enterprise is struggling to break free, and to improve upon, it is not surprising that values other than economic efficiency have not been explored. The danger in extending the range of instrumental values is that the theory becomes diffuse and indeterminate. Its predictive capacity may well disappear. The introduction of other values, even such long-established alternatives (or additional values) as distribution of income, is to unduly complicate the analysis, to make it less tractable and to descend to mere description. (See, for example, Casson who points out that equity requires a separate treatment from efficiency and such a treatment needs to beware of subjectivity [Casson 1979, p. 28]). The incorporation of values other than efficiency in the theory in a tractable manner is a major challenge to institutionalist approaches.

CONCLUSION

There is clearly a role for institutionalist elements to play in improving, extending and refining the current theory of the multinational enterprise. Indeed, the success of the internalisation approach has been partly the result of its incorporation of institutional variables. The task of taking this further is not an easy one. The theory must retain its determinacy and its predictive power and must not be overwhelmed by vague variables that degenerate into descriptive detail. Given the robust nature of the existing building blocks, there is scope for a more thorough going institutionalist examination of those areas, such as corporate culture, welfare implications, and alternative social values, which are currently imperfectly explored.

References

Axelrod, R. 1984. *The Evolution of Co-operation* (New York: Basic Books).
Buckley, Peter J. 1985a. 'New Forms of International Industrial Co-operation' in Peter J. Buckley and Mark Casson, *The Economic Theory of the Multinational Enterprise: Selected Papers* (London: Macmillan).
Buckley, Peter J. 1985b. 'The Economic Analysis of the Multinational Enterprise: Reading versus Japan?' *Hitotsubashi Journal of Economics* 26 (December): 117–24.
Buckley, Peter J. 1988. 'The Limits of Explanation: Testing the Internalisation Theory of the Multinational Enterprise', *Journal of International Business Studies* 19 (Summer): 181–93.
Buckley, Peter J. and Mark Casson. 1976. *The Future of the Multinational Enterprise* (London: Macmillan).
Buckley, Peter J. and Mark Casson. 1985. *The Economic Theory of the Multinational Enterprise: Selected Papers* (London: Macmillan).
Buckley, Peter J. and Mark Casson. 1988. 'A Theory of Cooperation in International Business' in *Cooperative Strategies in International Business*, ed. Farok Contractor and Peter Lorange (Lexington, Mass.: Lexington Books).
Buckley, Peter J. and Mark Casson. 1989. *The Future of the Multinational Enterprise*, paperback edition (London: Macmillan).
Buckley, Peter J. and Hafiz Mirza. 1985. 'The Wit and Wisdom of Japanese Management: An Iconoclastic Analysis', *Management International Review* 25 (1985): 16–32.
Casson, Mark. 1979. *Alternatives to the Multinational Enterprise* (London: Macmillan).
Casson, Mark. 1985a. 'The Theory of Foreign Direct Investment', in Buckley and Casson, *The Economic Theory of the Multinational Enterprise*.
Casson, Mark. 1985b. 'Entrepreneurship and the Dynamics of Foreign Direct Investment', in Buckley and Casson, *The Economic Theory of the Multinational Enterprise*.
Casson, Mark. 1987. *The Firm and the Market* (Oxford: Basil Blackwell).
Hymer, Stephen P. 1969. *The International Operations of National Firms: A Study of Direct Investment*. PhD. Diss., MIT (Cambridge, Mass.: MIT Press, 1976).
Kindleberger, C.P. 1969. *American Business Abroad* (New Haven: Yale University Press).
McClintock, Brent. 1988. 'Recent Theories of Direct Foreign Investment: An Institutionalist Perspective', *Journal of Economic Issues* 22 (June): 477–84.
Robinson, John. 1983. *Multinationals and Political Control* (Aldershot: Gower).
Rugman, Alan M., Donald J. Lecraw, and Laurence D. Booth. 1985. *International Business: Firm and Environment* (New York: McGraw Hill).

Schumpter, J.A. 1934. *The Theory of Economic Development* (Cambridge, Mass.: Harvard University Press).

Teece, David J. 1983. 'Technological and Organisational Factors in the Theory of the Multinational Enterprise', in *The Growth of International Business*, ed. Mark Casson (London: George Allen & Unwin).

Vernon, Raymond. 1971. *Sovereignty at Bay* (Harmondsworth: Penguin).

Vernon, Raymond. 1977. *Storm over the Multinationals: The Real Issues* (London: Macmillan).

6 Alliances, Technology and Markets: A Cautionary Tale

Peter J. Buckley

A number of recent attempts have been made to encompass significant developments in the world economy, relating to inter-firm agreements, particularly those centred on technological exchange and development. This chapter is an attempt to systematise an approach to such developments which enables rigorous analysis and to make certain distinctions crucial to clarification. The view it takes is that several disparate phenomena are encompassed in extant umbrella concepts and that enlightenment can be achieved by the use of appropriate analytical tools, organising concepts and the judicious use of Occam's razor.

The first section presents a suggestion for a conceptual structure appropriate to the analyses of technological alliances. The second discusses a number of important new elements which appear to be necessary if progress is to be made.

6.1 CONCEPTUAL STRUCTURE

There appear to be two clear and distinct methods of analysing alliances between firms. One is to identify two modes of allocating resources – the firm and the market, or the organisation and the market, and to identify firm-like behaviour and market-like behaviour in alliances or technology agreements. The second is to propose a third (or fourth) operational form variously identified as clan, alliance, network, or federation and to assign alliances to one or more of these forms.

Alliances have been added to what Richardson (1972) identified as the 'dense network of co-operation and affiliation by which firms are

This chapter was stimulated by a meeting of the 'Oligopolies and Hierarchies' Working group at Fondation de Royaumont, Asnières-sur-Ase, France, 20–23 May 1989. I would like to thank the other participants for their stimulating contributions, particularly the organiser/editor, Lynn Krieger Mytelka.

inter-related' (p. 833). It is, however, clear (i) that alliances need to be identified as a distinct and distinctive form of operation; (ii) that the term 'alliance' be reserved for only this type of institutional arrangement. Buyer–seller relationships, for instance, should not be placed in this category.

Cooperation across institutional boundaries is a feature of an alliance. This cooperation must stop short of merger. Ideally, it should be possible to specify the conditions leading to the creation of an alliance and the conditions leading to its demise or its changing into another form. However, this must not occur in a situation where all states of the world are possible. Limits to merger may thus be important factors in the creation of alliances which may be second-best solutions where the preferred form – merger (acquisition, amalgamation) – is ruled out by the existence of constraints.

Such distinctions must be empirically tractable. They must be able to separate observations of alliances uniquely from other mixed forms of collaboration. We may thus define an alliance as an 'interfirm collaboration over a given economic space and time for the attainment of mutually defined goals'. This definition has several important characteristics. (1) It covers only *inter-firm* agreements. Situations which are, or become, intra-firm are excluded. The essence of an alliance is operating across the boundaries of the firm. (2) The venture must be collaborative, that is, there must be some input of resources from both (if two) or all (if more) of the partners in the alliance. There is no implication that these inputs must be in any way equal. The case of equality of inputs will be a special case. (3) The alliance must be defined over a given economic space and time. It can thus range from local, regional or national to global. It can be defined in real time or until certain goals are reached, but will seldom (if ever) be indefinite. (4) An alliance will be defined for the achievement of certain goals. This may be a physical goal, set in terms of achieving a given output, it may be a market goal, such as achievement of a given market share, or it may be a technological or management objective. It is possible that misperception will occur or deception will be used in the establishment of these goals so that alliances may be perceptually asymmetrical and this aspect needs further clarification. For the moment we assume that all (both) partners have the same views of the objectives.

Is this definition exhaustive and does it exclude all collaborative forms which are not alliances? Agreement on goals excludes all non-purposive agreements. It also excludes buyer–seller relationships, subcontracting, countertrade agreements, licensing and franchising, barters and buybacks where the parties have to some degree opposing goals – the sellers to sell dear and the buyers to buy cheap.

This is not to go so far as to call such ventures cooperative, however.

Buckley and Casson (1988) attempted to define a non-trivial special case where cooperative behaviour took place. Cooperation was defined as 'co-ordination effected through mutual forbearance' (p. 32). Such cooperative behaviour *may* occur in alliances, but it is not necessarily present and is not a definitive condition of alliances. What is necessary is some agreement on goals and some reciprocity between partners. This may build into genuine cooperation either as an unintended consequence or through design but it is not necessary at the outset.

A number of factors will be conducive to the building of such alliances: (1) the possession of complementary assets; (2) similarity or congruence of goals, which may include the desire to reduce competition and (3) barriers to full integration: economic, political or legal.

Joint ventures

The economic theory of joint ventures as expressed by Buckley and Casson (1988, pp. 40–9) suggests that there are three key elements in the decision to set up a joint venture. The analysis proceeds assuming only two partners to the joint venture.

1. Joint ventures are preferred to arms-length trade because there is a net benefit from internalising a market in one or more intermediate goods and services flowing between the joint venture and the parties' other operations. This may be symmetrically motivated if the parties have the same motive for internalising the intermediate products, or it may be asymmetrical.
2. Each firms owns part of the joint venture rather than the whole of another facility. This may be explained by a variety of causes but depends on indivisibilities.
    a) If the joint venture produces a homogeneous output shared between the two partners or uses a homogeneous input jointly sourced by them, then the indivisibility is an economy of scale.
    b) If the joint venture generates two distinct outputs, one used by one partner and one by the other, then the indivisibility is an economy of scope.
    c) If the joint venture combines two different inputs each of which is contributed by just one of the parties, then the indivisibility is simply a technical complementary between inputs (a combination of diminishing marginal rate of technical substitution and non-decreasing returns to scale).
        Implicit in this 'search for indivisibilities' is the assumption that extra-managerial problems are encountered in joint-venture operations.

3. The existence of a joint venture rather than merger between the part-
    ners suggests that net disadvantages to merger exist. These may arise
    from managerial diseconomies (possibly related to the scale and diversity
    of the potential post-merger company), legal obstacles arising from
    antitrust policy or regulations on foreign ownership, constraints arising
    from the financial markets amongst other reasons.

Thus joint ventures can be explained by internalisation economies,
indivisibilities and obstacles to merger.

To return to the question – are joint ventures alliances? The answer is
yes. They involve inter-firm collaboration, have inputs from both parties
and are defined in terms of goals over a well-defined economic space. Joint
ventures thus are simply alliances cemented by equity holdings. Two classes
of alliances can be defined – equity alliances (joint ventures) and non-
equity alliances.

Alliances can thus be between firms linked in the value chain (*vertical*)
so long as this is not purely a buyer–seller relationship. They can be
between direct competitors producing essentially the same output (*horizontal*), or they can be cross-sectoral, between essentially unrelated companies. Each type of alliance has different implications for competition.

The question arises of the degree of independence of the firms in the
alliance. In Japan, for example, many vertical alliances will be members of
the same *keiretsu* or industrial group. Horizontal alliances may be between
members of the same trade association. Where the independence of firms is
questionable, empirical case-by-case judgement is necessary to answer the
question as to whether an arrangement is actually an *inter-firm* alliance.

Technology agreements

The arrangement where two companies come together to develop a particular
piece of technology or to investigate an area of basic research, is analogous
to the case of joint ventures above.

Technology: special issues

When the inputs and/or outputs transferred or developed within the alliance
are technology-based, many commentators have suggested that special
issues arise. The joint development of new technology in a technological
alliance is a further special case. It is in the area of technological development
that networking of alliances occurs. Concern over the proprietary nature of
technological development must be balanced against economies of scale
and scope in basic research facilities. The increasing 'critical mass' or
'minimum' efficient scale of basic research in a number of key

technological areas is attested to by a large amount of empirical research. The concentration of resources on key problems or bottlenecks in research across a number of organisations (including government ministries) is an approach favoured by the Japanese in a series of projects.

6.2 COMPETITIVE ISSUES

The establishment of alliances between firms has significant implications for competition. A class of 'strategic alliances' has been defined by some analysts as a term for inter-firm agreements which are intended to further the competitive position of participant firms. This has been taken further by others who infuse the term 'strategic' with the notion of 'opportunistic'. It is important to make sense of these terms and to use them in a neutral, rather than a loaded sense.

The competitive impact of alliances depends on the alternatives which are possible and feasible, and on the context. In terms of the analysis above, if the alternative to a purposive joint venture is two competing plants, then, if we go no further, such alliances reduce competition and are in essence exactly equivalent to a merger in the particular input or output which the joint venture produces. However, in efficiency terms, this ignores the benefits of the alliance in transaction cost savings (internalisation benefits) and it ignores the difficulties of overcoming the indivisibility leading to the alliance.

If the alternative to the alliance is two competing projects, then competition clearly suffers. However it is possible that this leads to a wastage of resources, duplication of effort and operation at suboptimal scale. Internalisation gains are forgone in attaining market gains and resources have to be supplied to both facilities to overcome indivisibilities.

Such speculation is essentially comparative–static in its terms of reference, attempting to compare the equilibrium outcome in the presence of an alliance with the equilibrium outcome(s) in the absence of the alliance. As such, it ignores competitive dynamics.

There are, of course, barriers to merger and to hostile takeover bids. These barriers vary by host country. Legal restrictions obviously vary (they vary widely, for instance, across the European Community) but so does the extent of family holdings (typical of Italy) and intra-group cross-holdings (typical of Germany and Japan). The extent to which there is a true market in company governance does therefore vary widely. In an extensive market, we can envisage a market in corporate control in which different management groups (or potential management groups) bid for control of corporate assets. These groups are backing their judgement against the market, based, perhaps, on their belief that under new management the existing assets could yield a greater return. In the absence of this first best solution, alliances may yield part of the same results.

Competitive dynamics

Alliances, by definition, are undertaken by existing firms. The alliance firms are in a competitive situation with other firms and are in certain cases in competition with each other prior to, and following the alliance. It is often the competitive process which is the key to initiating the alliance.

Global competition

Defensive alliances are often initiated by the threat of entry or actual entry by foreign competitors.

The role of information and learning

Arguments for alliances as improvements in resource allocation centre not only on indivisibilities and reduction of transaction costs but also as uncertainty-reducing devices (Jorde and Teece 1989). In periods of rapid changes, notably when technology is evolving rapidly, it is argued that purely market-based relationships between firms are insecure. Consequently, joint planning, e.g. of future input-sourcing, provides security against unforeseen market fluctuations. This argument for replacing the market by contract to avoid uncertainty is analogous to that of Coase (1937) in establishing a rationale for the firm itself. Again this argument needs support in the form of barriers to merger or full integration.

Political economy issues

In industries producing income-elastic goods for which there is an increasing demand in less developed countries (automobiles, pharmaceuticals, electronic products) several political economy factors favour alliances.

Many multinational firms which possess technical skills may not possess the adaptation skills necessary to service a growing developing country (or newly industrialising country) market. Such firms are therefore constrained to adopt market-servicing policies based not on wholly-owned direct investment but on licensing or alliances. Licensing may not be the optimal form of market-servicing because of its reliance on the market and because of well-known barriers to effective implementation of a licensing system

(Buckley and Casson 1976; 1985; Buckley and Davies 1980). The choice of a cross-national alliance with a host-country firm cemented possibly by joint equity ownership as a joint venture becomes attractive. If more than one foreign partner is involved then consortium arrangements may emerge (Buckley 1985).

The positive approach to alliances may well be reinforced by the attitude of the host country government. The government may restrict imports by tariff and quota arrangements and may resent foreign 'domination' as represented by wholly-owned foreign subsidiaries. This leaves the alliance as the best choice in these circumstances. (For a review of policies on joint ventures see the OECD Report *Competition Policy and Joint Ventures* [1986]).

Firms may thus develop, by accident or design, a network of alliances. There is likely to be a considerable learning effect in such a development. It is arguable that several firms have developed 'networking skills' in building up an international system of alliances. This may be a highly effective means of servicing fragmented world markets analogous to an optimal licensing system (Casson 1979) but arguably more effective because of the increased coordination possibilities arising from the use not only of market signals but also administrative commands through internal procedures and communications.

Cartels, collusion and networks

The literature on cartels is illuminating when considering the choice between formal or informal collusion and the integrated multiplant firm, of which the multinational enterprise is a special case. Casson (1985) suggests that the advantages of the integrated multiplant firm are greatest where monitoring of the behaviour of individual units is greatest and where the legal environment is most hostile to cartel arrangements.

Collusion is most likely to take place where demand is inelastic, buyers atomistic, sellers few and where there is little outside entry into the industry. The minimum efficient scale of operation is likely to be large, relative to the market. A cartel rather than an integrated multiplant firm is the more likely institution for implementing collusion when the product is homogeneous, economies of scale are absent, there is low capital intensity, static technology, the absence of innovation and a high risk of appropriation of foreign assets (Casson 1985).

Cartels may be viewed as non-equity alliances where the agreed objective is the restriction of output. Cartels are a further special case in that, in order to be effective, they must cover a large proportion of the industry, preferably the whole industry.

6.3 ALLIANCES IN PRACTICE

The analysis above suggests that alliances are a combination of three motives, any one of which may be dominant or dormant in particular circumstances. The three motives are: (1) complementary resources, (2) congruence of goals, possibly including restriction of competition and the erection or consolidation of entry barriers and (3) barriers to merger.

An important example of the interplay of these motives exists in the expansion of companies into new regions. The extensions, or intensification, of a common market as exemplified by the Single European Act, 1992 results in alliances in order to reap economies of scale and exploit complementary skills residing in firms of different nationalities, while avoiding the complications (legal, economic, political) of full merger. Similarly the opening-up of Eastern Europe is likely to lead to two distinct types of alliance – those between indigenous East European entities and foreign entrants and entirely foreign alliances, created expressly for the purpose of exploiting the new liberalised market. The first type will occur where local marketing and production skills are required and where legal regulations dictate. The second type will occur for large-scale projects with multiple purposes in typical consortium situations. The influence of economic de-regulation is therefore to intensify alliance activity.

Quantification

Attempts to quantify alliances are fraught with difficulty. First, there are problems of definition. As shown above, it is not easy to fix a definition which includes all alliances and only alliances. Second, primary data have to be collected. Many alliances are not publicly announced. Reporting of announcements may vary by country, industry, time of year and a host of other factors including the existence and reliability of trade journals. Third, it may not be possible to ascertain the nature of the inter-firm agreement and so it is unlikely that pure and homogeneous results are obtained.

Nevertheless, several databases have been constructed (for a review, see Chesnais 1988). These databases show an increasing trend in the formation of alliances, particularly in R & D-intensive or technology-intensive industries (although it should be borne in mind that these are the most researched and publicity-conscious industries!). Among the most numerous specific types of alliances are collaborative research and development, project-specific alliances (including those explicitly government sponsored), specialised firms (by function) seeking complementary assets and alliances in product-based and technology-based oligopolistic industries. As yet, it is impossible to give global figures or even pan-EC figures for alliances.

Specific instances of alliances

On the basis of previous studies, it is possible to analyse several alliances. However, in the absence of primary data collection, it is necessary to take on board the analysis of those who amassed the data. This may present hazards.

It should also be remembered that the number of alliances is large and increasing. The General Electric Co. (USA) also has more than 100 joint ventures (*Business Week*, 21 July 1986). One major purpose of these alliances is to spread research and development costs and thus risks. (See for example 'GE seeks partners to share cost of jet engine development' *The Financial Times*, 17 January 1990).

Problems of alliances

Coordination problems across the boundaries of firms are a major difficulty in the management of alliances. If the alliance is a transnational one – like Airbus Industries – then the component national management cultures may cause friction. Transnational alliances coordinated by government or public sector bodies may involve a twofold culture-clash. These difficulties may be more severe where they occur across firm boundaries than in a multi-national firm because the mechanisms of control are less direct and unified.

6.4 CONCLUSION

Alliances can be specified as a unique form of business organisation. An alliance can be defined as an interfirm collaboration over a given economic space and time for the attainment of mutually defined goals. A joint venture is a special case of an alliance where the collaboration is cemented by an equity link.

Care must be taken when examining the number of alliances and specific instances. Generally alliances occur where firms have complementary assets, congruence of goals and where there exist barriers to full integration. The competitive effects of alliances require careful case-by-case examination with attention paid to the feasible alternative.

References

Buckley, Peter J. 1985. 'New Forms of International Industrial Co-operation' in Buckley and Casson, op. cit.

Buckley, Peter J. and Mark Casson. 1976. *The Future of the Multinational Enterprises* (London: Macmillan).

Buckley, Peter J. and Mark Casson. 1985. *The Economic Analysis of the Multinational Enterprise* (London: Macmillan).

Buckley, Peter J. and Mark Casson. 1988. 'A Theory of Co-operation in International Business', in Farok J. Contractor and Peter Lorange (eds), *Co-operative Strategies in International Business* (Lexington, Mass.: Lexington Books).

Buckley, Peter J. and Howard Davies. 1980. 'Foreign Licensing in Overseas Operations: Theory and Evidence from the UK', in Robert G. Hawkins and A. J. Prasad (eds), *Technology Transfer and Economic Development* (Greenwich, Conn.: JAI Press).

Casson, Mark. 1979. *Alternatives to the Multinational Enterprise* (London: Macmillan).

Casson, Mark. 1985. 'Multinational Monopolies and International Cartels', in Buckley and Casson, op. cit.

Chesnais, François. 1988. 'Technical Co-operation Agreements Between Firms', *STI Review* (OECD), Vol. 4, December, pp. 51–120.

Coase, Ronald H. 1937. 'The Nature of the Firm', *Economica* (New Series), Vol. 4, pp. 386–405.

Jorde, Thomas M. and David J. Teece. 1989. 'Competition and Co-operation: Striking the Right Balance', *California Management Review*, Vol. 31, no. 3, Spring, pp. 25–37.

OECD. 1986. *Competition Policy and Joint Ventures* (Paris: OECD).

Richardson, G. B. 1972. 'The Organisation of Industry', *Economic Journal*, Vol. 82, pp. 883–96.

Part III

Multinational Enterprises in the World Economy

7 Joint Ventures in Yugoslavia: Opportunities and Constraints

Patrick F. R. Artisien and Peter J. Buckley

ABSTRACT

Yugoslavia's post-1965 economic policies have been directed towards opening the economy to foreign trade and encouraging inward investment in Joint Ventures. This research examines the opportunities and constraints facing Western multinational companies which invest in Joint Ventures in Yugoslav industry. The empirical evidence drawn from a sample of 42 West European and North American companies addresses itself to the formation and success of Joint Ventures, the route to foreign direct investment in Yugoslavia and motives and preferences for Joint Ventures to other forms of industrial cooperation.

This chapter is based on an empirical study of Western European and North American multinational companies which have invested in Yugoslav industry between 1968 and 1980. The first section examines the advantages and drawbacks of Yugoslavia as a host country for such ventures. The second section analyses the nature and overall pattern of Joint Ventures in Yugoslav industry, and the third section summarises the legal regulations governing such ventures. The fourth section summarises a detailed empirical analysis of 42 Joint Ventures, concentrating on their location decision, the degree of successful operation achieved, the foreign entrant's pre-Joint Venture dealings with Yugoslavia and the motives behind the decision to implement a Joint Venture.

PROFILE OF YUGOSLAVIA AS A HOST TO JOINT VENTURES

Yugoslavia displays the features of an economy at an intermediate stage of development between a less developed country and an advanced industrialised economy. On the one hand, rapid industrialisation and urbanisation combined with a low population growth in the postwar period have resulted in marked improvements in living standards: between 1965 and 1979, the growth in Gross Domestic Product averaged 6 per cent per annum. The ratio of investment to Gross Domestic Product at 28 per cent per annum was higher than that of any OECD country with the exception of Japan. As a result, Gross Domestic Product per capita reached a postwar peak of US $3034 in 1980.

Growth in real incomes was accompanied by structural changes in the sectoral distribution of the labour force: between 1953 and 1978 labour moved from the predominantly private-owned agricultural sector to the social sector, dominated by industry and services. In this period, the share of the labour force employed in agriculture declined from 69 per cent to 36.8 per cent, while employment in industry and services rose respectively from 10.9 per cent to 21.8 per cent and from 20.1 per cent to 41.4 per cent of the working population. Labour also left the country at a steadily increasing rate in the 1960s. The World Bank estimated that the number of Yugoslav workers temporarily employed abroad had risen from 138 000 in 1964 to 1.1 million in 1973.[1] Since 1974, however, a reduction of employment opportunities in Western Europe combined with the introduction of restrictive legislation governing the employment of foreign labour (particularly in West Germany and Switzerland) has resulted in more Yugoslav workers returning home than going abroad. The reduction in the outflow of labour has exacerbated Yugoslavia's domestic employment problem; in 1983 unemployment reached some 860 000 or 9 per cent of the total labour force.

Other key macro-economic indicators reveal a per capita Gross Domestic Product much below that of most OECD countries, a persistently adverse balance of payments, growing indebtedness and severe regional disparities in living standards. This predicament, shared by many less developed countries, was exacerbated in Yugoslavia by the political and economic constraints which the ideological break with the Cominform in 1948 imposed on economic development between 1950 and 1965.

Yugoslavia's trade structure since the Second World War has reflected its changing political alliance. Table 7.1 shows that Yugoslavia moved from heavy trade dependence on Comecon (51.6 per cent of its exports and 48.4 per cent of imports in 1948) to almost total reliance on Western Europe and North America during the period of the Cominform economic blockade (80.5 per cent of exports and 88.9 per cent of imports in 1953).

Yugoslavia resumed trade contacts with Eastern Europe in 1954 and gained observer status in Comecon ten years later. The post-1960 period led to fluctuating trading relations with the capitalist, socialist and less developed nations. Between 1960 and 1982 the share of Yugoslavia's exports to

OECD countries was almost halved, to a postwar low of 28.2 per cent, while exports to Comecon over the same period increased by over 1½ times, although this trend is now slowly being reversed (see trade figures for 1983). This illustrates, on the one hand, the continuing lack of competitiveness of Yugoslav goods in Western markets, and on the other, the choice of the easier Comecon option, typified by Yugoslav firms contracting to sell their entire output over a period of several years to East European buyers. The geographical distribution of imports has been more stable than that of exports, but displays the same trends: upward with Comecon, downward with OECD. Trade with the developing countries is relatively modest (18.4 per cent in 1983). In view of Yugoslavia's active participation in the nonaligned movement, of which many of its less developed trading partners are members, Yugoslav firms have not fully utilised their potential for opening new markets in the Third World.

The 1965 economic reforms marked the final phase of the transition to market socialism and proclaimed Yugoslavia's intention to integrate with

TABLE 7.1 *Distribution of Yugoslavia's foreign trade, 1948–1983 as a percentage of total trade*

	Exports								
Destination	*1948*	*1953*	*1960*	*1965*	*1970*	*1975*	*1980*	*1982*	*1983*
OECD countries of	42.9	80.5	52.1	42.3	55.9	35.6	37.4	28.2	33.4
which EEC	19.4	39.9	25.6	25.1	39.0	22.8	26.3	20.4	23.8
USA	2.7	14.0	6.9	5.7	5.3	6.5	4.4	3.0	3.5
Comecon	51.6	0.0	32.1	42.0	32.5	47.1	46.1	51.0	46.7
Developing countries	5.5	19.5	15.8	15.7	11.6	17.3	16.5	20.8	19.9
	100.0	100.0	100.0	100.0	100.0	100.0	100.0	100.0	100.0

	Imports								
Origin	*1948*	*1953*	*1960*	*1965*	*1970*	*1975*	*1980*	*1982*	*1983*
OECD countries of	43.9	88.9	58.9	54.1	67.8	60.7	52.9	51.2	46.2
which EEC	25.0	38.7	32.5	26.0	46.6	41.1	34.7	33.6	30.4
USA	3.5	34.4	10.7	14.8	5.6	5.4	6.7	6.3	6.4
Comecon	48.4	0.0	25.5	28.5	20.7	24.6	30.0	34.7	36.9
Developing countries	7.7	11.1	15.6	17.4	11.5	14.7	17.1	14.1	16.9
	100.0	100.0	100.0	100.0	100.0	100.0	100.0	100.0	100.0

Source : OECD Economic Survey, Yugoslavia (Paris, 1984).

the world economy: the Yugoslav market was to be opened to foreign competition in order to increase the industrial efficiency and competitiveness of Yugoslav enterprises. The Yugoslav authorities believed that private foreign investment would contribute towards this end by providing not only capital for domestic investment but also foreign exchange, modern technology and equipment, managerial and marketing skills, and a better knowledge of foreign markets with a view to expanding exports. There were two major considerations for giving preference to Joint Ventures with foreign firms. First, private foreign investment could not contravene the essence of workers' self-management, which ruled out both fully-controlled subsidiaries of foreign firms and joint-stock companies. Second, Yugoslavia's previous industrial cooperation with Western firms, mostly in the form of licensing, had not elicited the anticipated transfer of Western technology and know-how. Edvard Kardelj, then president of the Federal Assembly, pointed out in 1967 that:

> after seventeen years of experience, the Yugoslav authorities realized that foreign licensors and business consultants would probably not retain unflagging interest, and this would not maximise the assistance rendered, without having a substantial investment in the country.[2]

This illustrated the Yugoslav policymakers' belief that domestic entrepreneurial skills and productivity would be increased if a Joint Venture was made sufficiently attractive to the foreign investor so as to prompt him to take active and continuing participation in Yugoslavia's economic development programme.

THE NATURE AND PATTERN OF JOINT VENTURES IN YUGOSLAVIA

Between the adoption of the first foreign investment legislation in July 1967 and December 1980, the 199 Joint Ventures were signed to the value of 49 255 million dinars, of which the foreign participation amounted to 10 264 million dinars or 20.74 per cent of the total. Table 7.2 illustrates the preponderance of United States and EEC investments; the former, with 30 Joint Venture contracts, is the largest single investor with 3368 million dinars (32.8 per cent of total foreign capital). EEC investments originate mainly from the UK, West Germany and Italy (17.3 per cent, 11.0 per cent and 9.1 per cent of total foreign investment respectively); and the latter two rank among Yugoslavia's principal trading partners. Switzerland, Austria and Sweden (with 19, 7 and 6 contracts respectively) are the major non-EEC European investors.

Over this 13-year period, foreign investment inflows have been uneven: no contract was registered in 1967, and only 5 in 1968. Between 1968 and 1971, foreign investment averaged 276 million dinars per annum: the yearly average rose to 646 million dinars over the next two years, but fell to 315 million between 1974 and 1975. This temporary setback was linked to the international recession, and to an ideological split in Belgrade between those who saw foreign investment as essential to further economic development and a guarantee of Yugoslavia's independence, and the opponents of Western capital who feared that the power of foreign multinationals might threaten the autonomy of self-managed enterprises.[3] Further fluctuations were recorded in the second half of the decade: foreign investment

TABLE 7.2 *Joint Ventures between Yugoslav and foreign firms (1968–1980)*

Countries of origin	Number of contracts	Foreign capital invested (millions of dinars)	% of total foreign capital	% of total capital
USA	30	3 368.0	32.8	31.69
UK	12	1 777.8	17.3	12.78
Switzerland	19	1 637.1	16.0	28.48
FR Germany	52	1 123.0	11.0	13.92
Italy	31	937.6	9.1	21.65
France	11	290.0	2.8	25.07
Austria	7	254.1	2.5	14.19
Sweden	6	223.3	2.2	28.88
DR Germany	1	138.3	1.4	48.94
Luxembourg	4	126.0	1.2	24.65
Belgium	6	124.4	1.2	11.89
Netherlands	3	75.6	0.7	32.10
Czechoslovakia	1	59.6	0.6	44.21
India	1	43.9	0.4	20.00
Liechtenstein	8	40.8	0.4	14.81
Finland	1	19.1	0.2	16.05
Canada	1	8.3		25.00
Panama	2	7.1	0.2	49.17
San Marino	1	6.1		47.00
Denmark	2	4.3		42.00
	199	10 264.4	100.0	20.74

Source: Calculated from data communicated to the OECD by the Federal Committee for Energy and Industry, Belgrade. See OECD, Foreign Investment in Yugoslavia (Paris, 1982) p. 24.

TABLE 7.3 *Sectoral distribution of Joint Venture contracts in existence in 1980*

SIC description	1968–1975			1976–1980			1968–1980		
	Number of contracts	Total investment (millions of dinars)	Foreign investment in sector as % of total foreign investment	Number of contracts	Total investment (millions of dinars)	Foreign investment in sector as % of total foreign investment	Number of contracts	Total investment (millions of dinars)	Foreign investment in sector as % of total foreign investment
Food, drinks & tobacco	7	367	5.1	10	2 210	5.6	17	2 577	5.5
Chemicals & allied industries	17	1 510	23.5	10	4 293	25.1	27	5 843	24.7
Metal-using industries	10	398	6.3	7	1 871	4.5	17	2 269	4.9
Production of metals	5	5 791	10.7	7	16 427	34.5	12	22 218	29.2
Wood & paper industry	3	2 358	9.2	5	736	3.0	8	3 094	4.4
Transport equipment	9	2 053	24.9	8	3 807	15.2	17	5 860	17.3
Electrical engineering	8	868	3.3	6	527	2.0	14	1 395	2.3
Rubber industry	4	811	11.8	4	1 367	4.2	8	2 178	5.9
Other industries & activities	26	235	5.2	18	902	6.0	44	1 137	5.8
	89	14 387	100.0	75	32 145	100.0	164	46 532	100.0

Source : Direct communication to the OECD, Foreign Investment in Yugoslavia (Paris, 1982).

rose steeply to 2220 million dinars in 1976, followed by an equally large fall to 578 million in 1977. The introduction of a new law in 1978[4] making investment more attractive to the foreign Joint Venture partner resulted in an increase in the signing of new contracts: new investments amounted to 1300 million dinars in 1979 and to 1850 million in 1980.

An examination of existing contracts by industrial sector in Table 7.3 shows a concentration of foreign investment by industry: just under 25 per cent of the foreign capital inflow has gone into chemicals, 29 per cent into the production of ferrous and non-ferrous metals, and 17 per cent into the vehicle industry. A new orientation is discernible, however, in the sectoral distribution of foreign investments over time. Before 1976 foreign capital contributed mainly to the expansion and modernisation of existing industries (for example, the chemicals, transport and rubber industries), but now foreign investors concentrate on large-scale and complex projects in the basic industries (such as metal production). The foreign investors' initial interest in some traditional sectors – wood and paper, textiles and footwear, and agriculture and forestry – has since rescinded.

The distribution of Joint Ventures in Yugoslavia (see Table 7.4) shows that foreign investors prefer regions with a better infrastructure and a more developed industrial sector. This explains why 82.7 per cent of total foreign investment in existing contracts at the end of 1980 was concentrated in the

TABLE 7.4 *Distribution of Joint Ventures by republic and autonomous province (existing contracts)*

Location	Number of Joint Ventures	Foreign investment	
		millions dinars	% of total
Serbia Proper	42	4 233	41.8
Croatia	31	2 450	24.2
Bosnia-Herzegovina	28	1 275	12.6
Slovenia	39	1 069	10.6
Vojvodina	13	618	6.1
Kosovo	2	172	1.7
Macedonia	6	171	1.7
Montenegro	3	134	1.3
TOTAL	164	10 122	100.0

Source : Direct communication to the OECD, Foreign Investment in Yugoslavia (Paris, 1982).

110 *Studies in International Business*

economically more advanced republics of Serbia, Croatia and Slovenia and
in the autonomous Province of Vojvodina. Tax rebates available on reinvested profits and on investment in Yugoslavia's less developed southern
republics have failed to attract foreign investors; the less developed republics
of Bosnia-Herzegovina, Macedonia and Montenegro and the autonomous
Province of Kosovo account for only 39 contracts or 17.3 per cent of total
foreign investment, merely two-thirds of the share of Croatia alone.

LEGAL REGULATIONS

The legislation governing Joint Venture investment in Yugoslavia has been
enacted in four broad stages: the first law adopted in July 1967 established
the legal structure within which Joint Ventures between foreign and Yugoslav
enterprises became possible; subsequent laws and amendments in 1971,
1973 and 1976 were designed to consolidate the initial legislation by removing some of the formal and practical obstacles to increased foreign
investment. A law passed in April 1978 clarified the Yugoslav government's intent regarding foreign investors by broadening the range of Joint
Venture activities and by facilitating the conditions for profit transfer and
capital repatriation. Finally, a set of amendments passed by the Yugoslav
Parliament in November 1984 was introduced to remove the outstanding
disincentives to foreign investment by simplifying the cumbersome approval
procedure of previous Joint Venture laws.

The most significant provision of the 1967 law[5] is contained in Article
64, which allows the foreign partner only a minority interest in the Joint
Venture. The foreign investor invests in his Yugoslav partner and therefore
does not acquire ownership or property rights in a Yugoslav enterprise.
Foreign capital is in the form of deposits and is treated as guest capital,
which results in rights and activities being established at two levels.
According to Scriven:

> The partners exercise their rights through a Business Board with
> competences defined by the Joint Venture agreement, whilst workers of
> the Joint Venture enterprise continue to exercise their self-management
> rights through the organs prescribed by law for this purpose.[6]

Other provisions of the 1967 law allow the foreign Joint Venture partner to
capitalise the value of his asset contribution, which can take the form of
equipment, machinery, raw materials, technology, know-how and services.
His right to transfer profits and repatriate capital is subject to Yugoslavia's

foreign exchange laws; because these transfers can only be effected out of foreign exchange resources earned by the Joint Venture, the funds available for transfer are mostly a function of the Venture's exports. Under this legislation, the 'retention quota' available to the foreign partner for profit transfer amounted to only 7 per cent of export earnings.

According to Lamers,[7] a particularly objectionable provision of this legislation was the obligation put upon the foreign partner to reinvest 20 per cent of his post-tax profit or deposit it with a Yugoslav bank.

The provisions introduced in the 1971 Amendments[8] fell into four major categories. First, the foreign partner's obligation to reinvest 20 per cent of his post-tax profit was abolished. Second, the right to repatriate capital was more clearly defined: 33.3 per cent of the foreign exchange generated by the Joint Venture's exports and 10 per cent of annual depreciation charges became eligible for either profit transfer or capital repatriation. Thirdly, foreign investors received the guarantee that legal changes introduced after the date of registration would not affect adversely their position. Finally, a constitutional amendment introduced that same year vested in the republics the authority to tax the foreign investor's profit, resulting in lower taxes and more generous incentives for investments in Yugoslavia's less developed regions.

In spite of these provisions, some uncertainty remained. In the words of the OECD researchers:

> The legal picture remained nevertheless bewildering for the newcomer to the Yugoslav scene, and it was not easy for him to determine the scope and meaning of the many provisions with any degree of precision.[9]

An element of conciseness and greater accessibility was introduced in 1973 when the Yugoslav government consolidated the existing provisions into a single law.[10] This law gave the foreign investor an equal voice in the management of the Joint Venture and entitled him to a share of profits commensurate with his risk capital participation.

These benefits were temporarily counteracted in June 1976 by a Decree on Foreign Investment[11] issued by the Federal Executive Council, which transferred the decisions on day-to-day management from the Joint Management Board to the Workers' Council. The unpopularity of this measure in foreign business circles led to its repeal in 1978 by the Foreign Investment Law,[12] which has since received a mixed verdict from Western investors.[13]

The changes welcomed by the foreign investor include the elimination of the ceiling on imported equipment which was previously limited to one-third of the foreign partner's total investment. The Federal Secretariat for Foreign Trade and the Federal Committee for Energy and Industry reserve the right, however, not to grant an import licence if domestic inputs can be substituted to the same standards and in sufficient quantities. A second 'positive' provision exempts the foreign partner from updating patents and know-how transferred to the Joint Venture; under previous legislation, foreign participation could not consist of technology and know-how unless the Yugoslav partner had access to all subsequent technological improvements brought about by the foreign partner during the life of the contract. Thirdly, the new law excludes private foreign investment only for trade, insurance and social activities. This broader range of Joint Venture activities has led to new contracts being signed in banking and the exploitation of raw materials. Fourthly, profits accruing to the foreign investor may be paid in dinars, thus diminishing the need for exports. Easier conditions for profit transfer enable the foreign investor to repatriate 50 per cent of foreign exchange proceeds from exports, as compared with 33.3 per cent previously.

Among the provisions listed most frequently as restrictive by foreign investors are profit limitation, liability for losses, and the transfer of liquidation proceeds. The 1978 law stipulates that the Joint Venture contract must prescribe the maximum amount of profit available for distribution to the foreign partner; any excess must be reinvested or taken out as a reduction of the foreign partner's risk capital.

Furthermore, although the foreign partner's liability is limited to his share of the Joint Venture's risk capital (unless specified otherwise in the contract), both partners must cover losses within a legally set period early the following year, thus ruling out the possibility of carrying forward losses to the next financial year.

Finally, in the event of liquidation, as under previous legislation, the foreign investor is entitled to recoup the value of invested inputs; however, he has no claim to a share in the accumulated value of the joint undertaking.

Since 1980, a small number of well-publicised closures (notably the withdrawal of Dow Chemicals from the Joint Venture on the island of Krk[14] have cast doubt on some of the positive aspects of investing in Yugoslavia. Reinforcing the above, lobbies of Western businessmen (particularly West German chemical firms) have made strong amendments in Yugoslavia's foreign exchange legislation, trade mark and patent laws in the pharmaceuticals industry.[15]

The Yugoslav response came in November 1984 in the form of amendments to the 1978 legislation.[16] A 'positive' feature of the new law is the faster approval procedure: whilst under the 1978 legislation, registration could last one year or more. Article 50 now stipulates that the Federal Committee for Energy and Industry must inform the applicant of its decision within 60 days of receipt of the application. Second, Article 8 empowers the Joint Venture partners to borrow money to finance the joint business operations. The availability of finance from outside is enhanced further by Article 10 which allows foreign banks to become co-signatories to a Joint Venture. Third, profit ceilings have been lifted: although this measure should offer some encouragement to the foreign investor, Joint Ventures remain subject to the existing limitations on hard currency retention, namely that the repatriation abroad of the Western partner's share of profits is dependent on the Joint Venture's foreign currency earnings.

An interesting change brought about by the amendments is the abolition of the 49–51 per cent investment rule, traditionally presented as a guarantee to the self-management rights of the Yugoslav enterprise. It is doubtful, however, whether this measure will have little more than a psychological effect on foreign investors, who did not see the minority ownership requirement as a serious constraint. Other measures include a guarantee to the foreign partner that repayment of the value of his investment is inalienable (Article 25), an extension of the fields of activity in which Joint Ventures are allowed to operate to include health and recreation services (by implication an incentive intended to attract tourist companies) (Article 11), the abolition of the minimum capital investment previously required of the foreign investor, provisions which allow the foreign partner to audit the books of the Yugoslav enterprise in matters relating to the Joint Venture operations (Article 35) and the Yugoslav partner to discharge his obligations through service fees (Article 33).

The 1984 amendments have thus gone some way towards removing the most objectionable provisions of the 1978 law, but they fall short of the total liberalisation of profit transfer, which remains tied to the Joint Venture's capacity to earn hard currency mostly from exports.[17]

EMPIRICAL FINDINGS

The sample

The sample comprises 42 Western multinational companies from 13 countries which have invested in Joint Ventures in Yugoslavia between 1968 and 1980. It was estimated that these firms exceeded 25 per cent of the total population of operational Joint Venture contracts in December 1980 and accounted for approximately 23 per cent of the assets of such investors.

Interviews were conducted between March 1980 and January 1981 in four languages with senior executives from the Head Office of European firms, and European subsidiaries of North American companies, which in all sample cases conducted their Yugoslav operations from their European base.[18]

Table 7.5 shows the size of the 42 sample foreign firms. In Section A, using worldwide sales turnover as a measure of size, the sample splits fairly evenly at US $1000 million; 19 companies have sales of US $1000 million or over, whereas 23 countries have sales of below US $1000 million. An alternative measure of size – using numbers of employees – is shown in Section B. A high correlation seems to exist between the companies' worldwide sales turnover and number of employees. All 19 companies with sales of over US $1000 million employ 10 000 or more people; of the 23 companies below the US $1000 million sales threshold, 21 have a workforce of less than 10 000. Hence, at the outset, it seemed that the multinational company's size was neither an advantage nor a barrier to setting up a Joint Venture in Yugoslavia.

The 42 Joint Ventures show a great variety in foreign investment both in terms of absolute amounts and percentage participation in the risk capital (see Table 7.6). The smallest sum invested is 1.8 million dinars, and the largest investment put up by a single foreign partner amounts to 274 million dinars. In terms of percentage participation, the foreign partners' shares in the Joint Venture's risk capital range from 2 per cent to the legally permissible 49.9 per cent ceiling. The categorisation of foreign firms according to

TABLE 7.5 *Size of sample foreign firms (year ending December 1978)*

Section A		Section B	
Worldwide sales turnover (US $ million)	Number of firms	Total number of employees	Number of firms
Up to 100	14	Up to 1000	13
101 to 500	5	1001 to 5000	3
501 to 1000	4	5001 to 10 000	5
1001 to 5000	8	10 001 to 50 000	6
5001 to 10 000	5	50 001 to 100 000	5
Over 10 000	6	Over 100 000	10
TOTAL	42	TOTAL	42

Source : *Europe's 5,000 Largest Companies, 1980; The Times 1,000, 1979–1980; 1980–81.*

percentage participation in the risk capital was preferred to absolute amounts invested, for the following reasons: first, the former was deemed to reflect more closely the foreign partner's commitment to the activities of the Joint Venture, thus reducing the likely discrimination bias against smaller firms and/or firms with less extensive international operations. Second, it was found that the absolute amounts invested by foreign firms bore little or no relation to the parent company's total sales turnover or number of employees. Thirdly, the extreme diversity in absolute amounts invested (illustrated in Table 7.6, Section A) raised practical problems of classification because no correlation was apparent between absolute investments and percentage shares in risk capital.

Thus it seemed that two groups of firms might exist: Table 7.6 shows 20 firms with a percentage share below 25 per cent of the Joint Ventures' risk capital, and 22 firms whose shares range from 25.1 per cent to 49.9 per cent.

The 42 firms were also classified according to the major activity of the Joint Ventures, using the 1968 Standard Industrial Classification. Table 7.7 shows that the 42 Joint Ventures produce a wide variety of goods, the largest single group of Joint Ventures (15) is concentrated in the chemicals and allied industries; 11 are in the manufacturing of vehicles and tyres; 7 in engineering; 5 in metal manufacture; and 4 in food, drink, and tobacco products. Table 7.7 also shows that, in most standard industrial classifications under consideration, the sample is fairly evenly distributed among firms with above and below 25 per cent of the total risk capital; the only two exceptions are the chemicals and allied industries, where 12 of the 15

TABLE 7.6 *Foreign investment by absolute amount of participation and by percentage share of capital in Yugoslav Joint Ventures*

Section A		Section B		
Amount invested by foreign partner (millions dinars)	Number of Joint Ventures	Foreign partner's % share	Number of Joint Ventures	Sample distribution in current analysis
1.8 to 5.0	7	Up to 10.0	5	
5.1.to 10.0	6	10.1 to 20.0	10	20
10.1 to 25.0	14	20.1 to 25.0	5	
25.1 to 50.0	9	25.1 to 30.0	4	
50.1 to 100.0	4	30.1 to 40.0	7	22
Over 100.0	2	40.1 to 49.9	11	
TOTAL	42		42	42

TABLE 7.7 *Standard industrial classification (SIC) of sample firms*

SIC Order	SIC Description	Number of firms	Producer goods	Intermediate products	Consumer goods	Commitment to Joint Ventures' risk capital		Year of establishment of Joint Venture
						Above 25%	Below 25%	
III	Food, drink & tobacco	4	–	–	4	1	3	1971; 1972; 1976; 1980
V	Chemicals & allied industries	15	4	4	7	12	3	1970; 1971; 1971; 1972; 1972; 1972; 1973; 1973; 1973; 1973; 1973; 1973; 1976; 1978; 1979;
VI	Metal manufacture	5	4	1	–	1	4	1972; 1974; 1974; 1977; 1979;
VII	Mechanical engineering	5	5	–	–	2	3	1971; 1973; 1973; 1974; 1979;
VIII	Instrument engineering	1	–	–	1	–	1	1973;
IX	Electrical engineering	1	1	–	–	–	1	1972;
XI	Vehicles	6	–	2	4	4	2	1968; 1969; 1970; 1972; 1975; 1977;
XIV	Other manufacturing industries (tyres)	5	–	5	–	2	3	1971; 1972; 1973; 1973; 1979;
		42	14	12	16	22	20	

foreign firms have invested above 25 per cent of the Joint Ventures' risk capital, and the metal manufacturing industries, where four of the five foreign partners have a below-25 per cent share of total capital.

Lastly, Table 7.7 shows the year of establishment of the Joint Ventures and a breakdown into producer, intermediate and consumer goods.

The countries of origin of sample foreign investors (see Table 7.8) are very similar to Yugoslavia's main foreign trade partners: investors from the USA, the Federal Republic of Germany, Italy and Austria make up 21 of the 42 sample firms or 68.0 per cent of the sample's total foreign investment. It is worth noting that although US investment is post-1973 and encompasses only four contracts, it equals the combined investments from Italy, the Federal Republic of Germany and Austria (17 contracts in total). This illustrates a preference for investment in fewer but larger projects in the capital-intensive vehicle, tyre and chemicals industries. Conversely, West German, Italian and Austrian investments are spread over a longer period (the average and median age of combined West German, Italian and Austrian ventures being 9.1 and 9.5 years respectively compared with 5.2 and 5.0 years for the American ventures) and show a greater range, both in industrial classification and size.

The distribution of sample firms by regions indicates the foreign

TABLE 7.8 Countries of origin of sample firms

Country of origin	Amounts invested (millions dinars)	Percentage of foreign investment	Number of contracts
USA	818.6	35.4	4
UK	438.0	19.0	9
Italy	282.3	12.2	4
FR Germany	235.4	10.2	8
Austria	235.2	10.2	5
Finland	84.5	3.7	1
Netherlands	53.5	2.3	2
Switzerland	49.1	2.1	2
Belgium	48.5	2.1	2
Sweden	33.7	1.4	1
France	19.2	0.8	1
Canada	8.3	0.4	1
Denmark	4.3	0.2	2
TOTAL	2310.6	100.0	42

investors' preference for the economically more developed republics of Slovenia, Croatia and Serbia, as reported in Table 7.4.

In terms of size, industry, country of ownership and location in the host country, a comparison of the description of the sample with that of the overall population shows that the sample is representative.

The success of Joint Ventures

In view of the heterogeneous nature of the sample (in terms of size, industrial classification, nationality and location of the investment), no single, arbitrarily determined indicator of success was thought to adequately measure the performance level of the 42 respondents. Instead, they were asked to list the objectives of their participation in Joint Ventures with Yugoslav enterprises. The results in Table 7.9 show that the predominant objectives were growth (33 firms), profitability (27 firms), and exports (26 firms), which together with the firms' own perception of overall performance in Yugoslavia make up the success criteria used in the final part of this chapter to assess the route and motivation of firms which have set up production in Yugoslavia.

In the existing literature, the most often quoted measure of performance is profitability. This is based on the assumptions first, that overseas investment would normally be undertaken to secure higher profits than could be achieved through domestic expansion; secondly, that superior profits are the 'just reward' for incurring greater risks in a foreign environment; and finally, that foreign investment implies the possession of a competitive advantage in a foreign market to compensate for the better knowledge by indigenous firms of local market conditions.

In order to test these premises, all the sample companies were asked to

TABLE 7.9 *Firm's listing of performance objectives*

Response	Number of firms*
Growth	33
Profitability	27
Exports	26
Increased sales in Yugoslavia	6
Quality of product	3
Information withheld on confidential grounds	6

* Total greater than sample total of 42 because of multiple responses.

compare the profitability of their operations in Yugoslavia with those at home.[19] The inference from Table 7.10 (Section A) is that firms appear to have forgone optimising profits in Yugoslavia.

However, further discussion indicated that, besides the relatively high proportion of respondents who withheld information on confidential grounds (9), firms were not dissatisfied with their performance in Yugoslavia, but feared that disclosure of profits might raise the sensitive issue of 'economic exploitation' by foreign capitalists of the resources of a socialist country. This prompted a comparison of profitability in Yugoslavia with that in other less developed countries. The answers in Table 7.10 (Section B) show that only 6 firms (14.2 per cent of the sample) perceived their operations in Yugoslavia as less profitable than in other less developed countries. The inference from the above table is that foreign investments in Yugoslavia are on the whole less profitable than home-based investments, but as profitable as investments in other less developed countries.

The reasons given by firms for accepting lower profits in Yugoslavia than on similar home-based investments were twofold. First, the firms' global investment policy in Yugoslavia and Eastern Europe: having set themselves the multiple objectives of profitability, growth and exports, the majority of respondents did not wish to forgo the medium- and long-term benefits of an enlarged market solely for the purpose of short-term superior profits.[20] Secondly, the host country's constraints in the form of legal restrictions on the profitability of foreign firms, price controls forcing firms to sell at controlled prices on the Yugoslav market while importing inputs at world prices, and the fragmented Yugoslav market whereby a Joint Venture trying to sell in another republic may find that a parallel industry has already saturated the local market.

Finally, the respondents were asked whether on the whole the project's return on investment had reached their expectations: 23 companies (55 per cent of the sample) were satisfied with the rate of return on capital employed, whereas only 13 companies (30 per cent of the sample) thought that the return on investment was below expectations.

Further analysis of the evidence revealed that, of the 18 companies whose Yugoslav operations were less profitable than similar home-based operations, 10 thought that the return on capital invested in Yugoslavia had reached their expectations; and only 4 firms described the return on investment as below expectations. This suggests that financial results in Yugoslavia were set at a lower level than similar projects at home, and strengthens the argument that non-profit objectives played an important part in the firms' assessment of performance. Secondly, notwithstanding lower profit targets,

TABLE 7.10 *Relative profitability at home, in Yugoslavia, and in other less developed countries*

Section A	Number of firms	Section B	Number of firms
Operations in Yugoslavia are more profitable than home-based operations	4	Operations in Yugoslavia are more profitable than operations in other less developed countries	3
Operations in Yugoslavia are as profitable as home-based operations	8	Operations in Yugoslavia are as profitable as operations in other less developed countries	11
Operations in Yugoslavia are less profitable than home-based operations	18	Operations in Yugoslavia are less profitable than operations in other less developed countries	6
Answer withheld on confidential grounds	9	No experience in other less developed countries	10
Too early to comment	3	Information withheld on confidential grounds	9
Total	42	Too early to comment	3
		Total	42

the 23 firms' favourable assessment of return on capital suggests that a majority of firms were financially successful.

A second primary performance objective listed by sample firms was growth: 33 companies had expanded and 29 respondents had concrete plans to expand the physical capacity of operations in Yugoslavia; among the 13 firms which had no plans for expansion are included the 7 respondents whose operations in Yugoslavia were too recent for growth to be a relevant concern.

A third objective listed by 26 of the 42 companies was export performance: in the wake of setting up the Joint Venture, 30 firms (71 per cent of the sample) increased their exports to Yugoslavia, thus strengthening the evidence for the 'presence' principle, put forward by Newbould, Buckley and Thurwell,[21] who, in their study of smaller UK companies investing overseas, concluded that the establishment of an overseas production subsidiary acted as a gesture of goodwill to which residents responded not only by buying from the overseas subsidiary but also by increasing purchases from the parent company. This finding illustrates the emphasis placed by

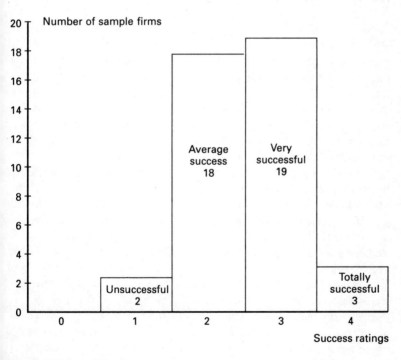

FIGURE 7.1 *Overall level of success*

the foreign investor on opening new markets in Yugoslavia.

Finally, in order to strengthen the robustness of the aforementioned criteria of success, it seemed pertinent to question each company about its own perception of overall performance in Yugoslavia. The results indicate overwhelmingly that companies' objectives were fulfilled: 40 firms either met or exceeded their objectives. This was confirmed by the question, 'With the benefit of hindsight, do you think that your decision to invest in Yugoslavia rather than to expand at home or to invest elsewhere was the correct tone?', to which 35 respondents replied in the affirmative.

The four elements of successful operation–profitability, growth, export success and fulfilment of expectations – are rated on a five-point scale (0–4) and a mean is taken. This crude procedure gives an overall success rating as shown in Figure 7.1 Three firms were rated 4 on each criterion and are labelled 'totally successful'; the other firms are distributed as shown. Overall, the sample is biased toward successful operation with only two firms being rated 'unsuccessful'.

The route to Joint Venture in Yugoslavia

Yugoslavia's need for technology and managerial expertise goes back well before the introduction of the 1967 foreign investment law. Prior to this legislation, Yugoslav enterprises had entered into three types of agreements with foreign firms: importing and exporting, the purchase of industrial property rights (licences, trade marks and patents), and long-term specialisation and cooperation in production (including contracts for co-production and mutual deliveries of semi-manufactured and finished products, subcontracting payment by end-product of the equipment supplied, joint marketing and research and development).[22]

Table 7.11 shows that past contacts with Yugoslav enterprises have affected the sample foreign firms' decision-making process: only 5 of the 42 companies had no previous association with Yugoslavia, and followed the 'direct route' with the least opportunities for assessing the business environment within which the investment would become operative. Lack of previous association would amount to the initial caution among these firms, four of which contributed less than 25 per cent of the Joint Venture's total risk capital. The levels of success achieved by the firms vary from very successful to unsuccessful and the group's mean success rating is 1.9.

The most popular route – consisting of exports and imports with Yugoslavia prior to setting up the Joint Venture – was followed by 20 firms, whose mean success rating was 2.5, or 0.6 higher than that of companies following the 'direct route'.

Table 7.11 *Route to Joint Ventures in Yugoslavia*

Route	Mean success rating	Total number of firms	Commitment to Joint Ventures' risk capital	
			Above 25%	Below 25%
Home operations – Joint Venture (direct route)	1.9	5	1	4
Home operations – exports, imports – Joint Venture	2.5	20	11	9
Home operations – exports, imports – licensing – Joint Venture	2.6	16	9	7
Home operations – exports, imports – licensing – long-term specialisation and cooperation in production – Joint Venture	2.0	1	1	–
TOTAL		42	22	20

The second most popular route was followed by 16 firms and involved two intermediate steps between home operations and the Joint Venture, namely exporting and importing as well as licensing property rights to the Yugoslav enterprise. Firms in this group recorded 'totally successful', 'very successful', and 'average success' ratings, leading to a mean success rating of 2.6. It is worth observing that the mean success rating increases as more steps are included along the route to setting up the Joint Venture, suggesting that the accumulation of experience and the step-by-step approach improve the chances of success.

The 'full route', including the above-mentioned intermediary steps and long-term specialisation and cooperation in production, was followed by only one firm. Two major factors account for the unpopularity of this route: first, most foreign firms under consideration already had some experience of licensing either in Yugoslavia or in Eastern Europe and were not initially attracted to Yugoslavia's experiment with a new form of industrial cooperation. In the 1960s the foreign firms preferred licensing to, rather than partnerships with, Yugoslav enterprises. Secondly, from the Yugoslav enterprises' viewpoint, long-term specialisation and cooperation in production agreements were not sufficiently geared to the acquisition of modern technology. Like their Western counterparts, but for different reasons, Yugoslav enterprises which entered into negotiations with foreign firms before 1967 had a clear preference for licensing agreements. (Figure 7.2 summarises the five routes in diagrammatic form.)

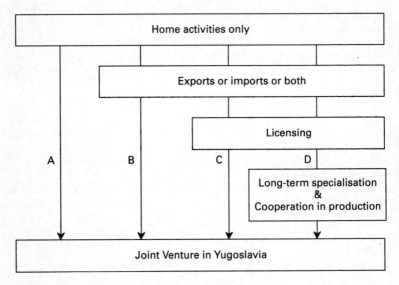

FIGURE 7.2 *Routes to a Joint Venture in Yugoslavia*

Because the majority of sample companies had experienced some form of trade and industrial cooperation with Yugoslav enterprises prior to setting up the Joint Venture, motives for preferring a Joint Venture investment were sought. Table 7.12 shows that for 13 firms, the choice was related to Yugoslavia's economic transformation in the late 1960s and 1970s. During this period the Yugoslav government adopted the view that licensing and cooperation in production and specialisation had not developed the necessary entrepreneurial skills and productivity to fulfill the economy's primary objectives of faster industrialisation, greater competitiveness in Western markets, and a reduction in the deficit on the balance of payments. After the introduction of a series of largely unsuccessful import-substitution and export measures, the Yugoslav authorities embarked on a policy of active encouragement of Joint Ventures by offering favourable terms and guarantees to the foreign investor.[23] Against this background, foreign firms were attracted by the opportunity to exploit more fully the Yugoslav market, a second motive mentioned by 12 respondents for setting up the Joint Venture.

A third motive for preferring a Joint Venture agreement (mentioned by 9 firms) was to improve the working relationship with the Yugoslav

TABLE 7.12 *Motives for preferring a Joint Venture*

Response	Mean success rating	Total number of firms*	Commitment to Joint Ventures' risk capital	
			Above 25%	Below 25%
Internal developments in Yugoslavia's socioeconomic system	2.7	13	2	11
To achieve further exploitation of the market	2.6	12	11	1
As a means of improving working relationship with partner	2.7	9	4	5
To facilitate technology transfer	2.4	8	5	3
To achieve greater participation in decision-making	3.1	8	4	4
Most suitable vehicle for business expansion at the time	2.2	6	5	1
Tariffs and quotas	2.3	4	3	1
Prospects of greater profits	3.0	3	1	2
To increase sales	2.0	3	3	–
Attractive proposition at the time	2.5	2	1	1
To overcome Yugoslav enterprise's hard currency shortage	4.0	2	–	2
To reduce amount of bureaucracy	2.0	1	–	1

* The total is greater than the sample total of 42 because of multiple responses.

enterprise in order to create a better investment climate. The impression gained from these respondents was that a Joint Venture provided greater motivation and opportunity for contact between partners than did a licensing agreement,[24] and that the medium- and long-term benefits derived from such a strengthened relationship outweighed the multinational companies' traditional insistence on control through wholly-owned subsidiaries or on above 50 per cent shares in equity capital. Among other motives frequently quoted were the desire to participate in the management of the Joint Venture on a direct and continuing basis, and to facilitate the transfer of technology to the Yugoslav enterprise.

Of the 18 firms (12 + 6) whose primary motivation for entering into a Joint Venture was to further the exploitation of the Yugoslav market and to expand business, 16 (11 + 5) invested above 25 per cent of the total risk capital (in 7 cases, the legal maximum of 49.9 per cent). This illustrates the aggressive policy of respondents and contrasts with the below 25 per cent risk capital commitment of 11 of the 13 respondents who chose the defensive approach and conformed to Yugoslavia's internal developments.

In terms of success, most groups display a mean success rating above average. The 8 respondents whose primary aim was to increase participation in decision-making have an average rating of 3.1, or 'very successful'.

Motivation for Joint Venture investments

The 42 companies were asked to give the motives for their investment in Yugoslavia: between two and four reasons were given which were classified in Table 7.13 into 'aggressive' and 'defensive' motives, using Root's definition.[25] Although the reasons enumerated are extremely varied, 53 of the 74 motives (or 72 per cent) fall within the aggressive category, which shows that over two-thirds of all sample firms invested in Yugoslavia in order to exploit either a present or an anticipated opportunity more effectively than was possible with exports or a different form of industrial cooperation. Table 7.13 also shows that market-induced motives predominate (32 firms). These firms' perception of opportunities for the exploitation of the Yugoslav and Comecon markets is reflected in their commitment to the risk capital of the Joint Ventures: 20 of the 32 companies invested a share of over 25 per cent of the Joint Venture's risk capital – 10 between 40.0 per cent and 49.9 per cent.

Among the company-induced aggressive motives, the largest single group of replies (8) concentrates on the need to develop manufacturing in Yugoslavia, and is related to a second motive, namely the desire to sell equipment and technology to Yugoslavia (3 firms). Both motives coincide with the

TABLE 7.13 *Motives for investing in Yugoslavia*

Motives	Mean success rating	Total number of firms*	Commitment to Joint Ventures' risk capital	
			Above 25%	Below 25%
Aggressive				
A. Market-induced				
1. Market opportunity in Yugoslavia	2.3	19	14	5
2. Market opportunity in Eastern Europe	2.3	9	5	4
3. Market opportunity in Middle East	2.0	2	1	1
4. To bring about direct control over marketing	4.0	2	–	2
		32	20	12
B. Company-induced				
1. To develop manufacturing in Yugoslavia	2.9	8	3	5
2. To increase sale of company's equipment and technology to Yugoslavia	2.0	3	1	2
3. To secure earnings from licences to Yugoslav enterprises	2.3	3	2	1
4. To obtain a superior profit	3.0	2	1	1
5. To improve quality of Yugoslav product	2.5	2	1	1
6. To achieve greater control over execution of project	3.0	1	–	1
7. To achieve greater control over sale of product	3.0	1	1	–
8. Source of raw materials	3.0	1	–	1
		21	9	12
Sub-total		53		
Defensive				
A. Market-induced				
1. To protect an existing market	2.5	12	9	3
2. To meet Yugoslav partner's requirements	2.7	3	2	1
3. To counter increasing Yugoslav competition	3.0	2	–	2
4. To safeguard company's interests	3.0	1	–	1
5. To create a favourable local working environment	3.0	1	–	1
6. Because of full capacity at home	3.0	1	–	1
		20	11	9
B. Company-induced				
1. Diversification of risk	2.0	1	1	–
Sub-total		21		

128 *Studies in International Business*

Yugoslav enterprise's policy to develop home-based manufacturing concurrently with the import of foreign technology and industrial know-how.

Among the 21 defensive motives the market influence also predominates: only one firm stated the company-induced diversification of risk as a factor of importance. The need to protect an existing market, at home or abroad, is the prevailing defensive motive (12 firms). For another three respondents, the need to acquiesce to the Yugoslav enterprise's requirements for joint cooperation, albeit initially defensive, was interpreted as a positive step toward protecting a market because the Joint Venture enabled the foreign company to exercise a degree of influence on the production, marketing and pricing policies of a particular product. The emphasis which investors have placed on market opportunities prompts the conclusion that political and business risks have not been a major obstacle to investing in Yugoslavia.

CONCLUSIONS

The evidence suggests that foreign investors in Yugoslavia have by and large fulfilled their pre-investment expectations. This finding is confirmed by other questions designed to crosscheck this result.[26] The identification by sample firms of several performance objectives (profitability, growth and exports) demonstrates that multinational enterprises investing in Yugoslavia follow a multiple- rather than single-objective strategy. The acceptance of lower profitability in Yugoslavia than on other foreign investments was compensated by the increase in exports to and enlarged markets in both Yugoslavia and Eastern Europe.

As for the route to the Joint Venture, the experiences of the 42 firms confirm 'common business sense': firms which took a step-by-step approach including intermediate stages such as exporting, importing and licensing, were more successful than those which followed a more direct route. This suggests that information gathered at each step of the cooperation was used beneficially to reappraise the next step of the investment policy.

The method of entry into the Yugoslav market was predominantly determined by the internal conditions prevailing at the time: the foreign firm's readiness to forgo a preference for total ownership and to adapt to the requirements of the host country illustrates a degree of flexibility prompted by market and growth criteria rather than by the profit motive.

Finally, although particular reasons apply to individual companies, aggressive investment predominates and is the major motivation for selecting

Yugoslavia as an investment location; the perception by sample firms of opportunities for expansion resulted in a greater percentage investment in the Joint Ventures' risk capital.

Notes

1. Schrenk, M., C. Ardalan, and N. Tatawy, *Yugoslavia: Self-Management Socialism*. A World Bank Country Economic Report. (Baltimore: The Johns Hopkins Press, 1979), pp. 244–85.
2. Quoted from an interview in *Borba* on 19 March 1967 by R. B. Glickman and M. Sukijasović, 'Yugoslav Worker Management and Its Effect on Foreign Investment,' *Harvard International Law Journal*, Vol. 12, no. 2, Spring 1972.
3. See Scriven, J. G. 'Yugoslavia's New Foreign Investment Law', *Journal of World Trade Law*, March/April 1979; and Artisien, P. F. R. and S. Holt, 'Yugoslavia and the E.E.C. in the 1970s', *Journal of Common Market Studies*, Vol. XVIII, no. 4, June 1980.
4. 'Law on investment of foreign persons' capital in domestic organizations of associated labour', *Službeni List S. F. R. Jugoslavije*, No. 18, April 1978.
5. For the full text of the law, see *Službeni List S. F. R. Jugoslavije*, No. 31, 19 July 1967.
6. J. G. Scriven, *JWTL*, p. 96.
7. E. A. A. M. Lamers. *Joint Ventures Between Yugoslav and Foreign Enterprises* (Tilburg University Press, 1976), pp. 158–59.
8. *Službeni List S. F. R. Jugoslavije*, No. 34, June 1971.
9. OECD, Foreign Investment in Yugoslavia, Paris, 1974, p. 9.
10. *Službeni List S. F. R. Jugoslavije*, No. 22, April 1973.
11. *Službeni List S. F. R. Jugoslavije*, No. 26, 18 June 1976.
12. *Službeni List S. F. R. Jugoslavije*, No. 18, April 1978.
13. The assessment of the 1978 law that follows is based on comments from the 42 sample foreign investors and on a survey of West German executives held under the joint auspices of the Berlin Management Education Institute and the West German Federal Office for Foreign Trade Information (see *Business Eastern Europe*, Vol. 7, nos. 45, 46, 47, November 10–24, 1978).
14. See *The Financial Times*, 2 December 1982, and *Business Eastern Europe*, Vol. XI, no. 49, 3 December 1982.
15. Memorandum zu den Problemen des Technologietransfers nach Jugoslawien unter besonderer Berucksichtigung der chemischen and pharmazeutischen Industrie. Frankfurt-am-Main, 2 September 1980.
16. The law on investment of resources of foreign persons in domestic organizations of associated labour (revised text, 27 November 1984), Federal Secretariat for Information, Belgrade, 1985.
17. For a fuller discussion of the 1984 amendments, see Artisien, P. F. R. and P. J. Buckley, 'Two views of foreign investment in Yugoslavia: the Western firm and the Yugoslav enterprise,' *Journal of World Trade Law*, Vol. 19, no. 5, 1985.

18. In the sample composition described below, the names of participants are omitted, as a pledge of confidentiality was made to each respondent.

19. Profitability in Yugoslavia is measured after taking account of distortions introduced by transfer prices and after deducting royalties and fees payable to the foreign partner.

20. The absence of superior profits among the motives of firms investing overseas has also been reported by A. M. Mathew, 'Recent Direct Investment in Australia by First Time U.S. Investors' (unpublished PhD Thesis, University of Bradford, 1979, p. 136), who also quotes the findings of D. T. Brash, *American Investment in Australian Industry*, Harvard University Press, Cambridge, MA, 1966, p. 40, and B. L. Johns, 'Private Overseas Investment in Australia: Profitability and Motivations', *The Economic Record*, Vol. 43, no. 102, June 1967, 233–6.

21. Newbould, G. D., P. J. Buckley, and J. Thurwell, *Going International, The Experience of Smaller Companies Overseas* (London: Associated Business Press, 1978), pp. 26–9.

22. For details, see P. F. R. Artisien, 'Joint Ventures in Yugoslav Industry', PhD Thesis, University of Bradford, 1982, pp. 80–90; a revised version was published as P. F. R. Artisien, *Joint Ventures in Yugoslav Industry*, (Gower: Aldershot and Brookfield, Vermont, 1985. See also P. F. Cory, 'Industrial Cooperation, Joint Ventures and the MNE in Yugoslavia', in A. Rugman (ed), *New Theories of the Multinational Enterprise* (London: Croom Helm, 1982).

23. Artisien, P. F. R., 'Belgrade's closer links with Brussels', *The World Today*, Vol. 37, no. 1, January 1981, 29–38.

24. This concurs with the findings of P. Killing, 'Technology Acquisition: Licence Agreement v. Joint Venture', *Columbia Journal of World Business*, Vol. XV, no. 3, Fall 1980; United Nations Economic Commission for Europe, *Promotion of Trade through Industrial Cooperation: Results of an Inquiry*. Trade R373, add. 2, 18 September 1978; and I. Fabinc, 'Institutional Features of the Transfer of Technology in Yugoslavia', Workshop of East–West Economic Interaction, Vienna Institute of Comparative Economic Studies, Baden, 3–7 April 1977.

25. In Root's terminology, a company demonstrates an aggressive strategy when it 'invests in a foreign country in order to exploit present and anticipated market opportunities more effectively than is possible through direct exports or other arrangements.' Conversely, a defensive strategy is followed 'when a primary motivation behind an investment is to hold on to a foreign market that can no longer be exploited by direct exports from the parent company's country'. See F. R. Root, 'U. S. Business Abroad and the Political Risks', *M. S. U. Business Topics*, Vol. 16, no. 1, Winter 1968, 74.

26. Artisien, 1982, 'Joint Ventures in Yugoslav Industry'.

8 Swimming Against the Tide? The Strategy of European Manufacturing Investors in Japan

Hafiz Mirza, Peter J. Buckley, and John R. Sparkes

THE OUTWARD URGE[1]

The last two decades have witnessed the internationalisation of the Japanese economy at a spectacular pace (see Table 8.1). In the 1970s, this process was especially evident in the rapid expansion of visible and invisible trade (both exports and imports); but in the 1980s, partly as a consequence of this trading success, the baton has passed to international investors and financial institutions. Table 8.1 shows that long-term capital outflows from Japan (be these direct investment, portfolio investment, or international bank loans) soared over the period between 1980 and 1986. This expansion overseas is increasingly aggressive, e.g. in 1986, Japanese takeovers in the USA exceeded US$2 billion in value,[2] and there is no sign of a slowdown. The Export–Import Bank of Japan predicts a further expansion in outward foreign direct investment;[3] and the outflow of long-term capital from Japan during 1987 (at US$170 billion) boosted the stock of such foreign assets by 36 per cent (the 1986 stock was US$476 billion).[4]

Of course, the surge in Japanese capital outflows is not unique, and a cursory examination of the net international capital flows of nine industrialised economies (Table 8.2) reveals that some countries are investing abroad at a very rapid pace.[5] However, it is also clear that Japan is in a league of its own,[6] with a net long-term capital outflow of US$284.6 billion during the period between 1980 and 1986. This situation is due to a variety of factors including (a) the appreciation of the yen by 61 per cent between 1980 and 1986 (Table 8.1); (b) a high savings rate combined with non-expansionary economic policies in the domestic market; (c) an increased institutional and corporate awareness of overseas opportunities which can be exploited through recently-acquired international managerial

131

Studies in International Business

TABLE 8.1 *The internationalisation of the Japanese economy*
(US$ billions, except where stated)

Item	Value				Expansion (%)[a]	
	1970	1980	1985	1986	'80/70	'86/80
Visible trade						
Exports	19.3	129.8	174.0	205.6	572	58
Imports[b]	18.9	140.5	129.5	126.4	643	−10
Net	0.4	−10.7	44.5	79.2		
Invisible trade						
Exports	4.0	31.5	45.6	53.5	687	70
Imports	5.8	42.8	50.6	58.0	638	36
Net	−1.8	−11.3	−5.0	−4.5		
Foreign direct investment						
Outward	0.4	2.4	6.5	14.1	500	488
Inward	0.1	0.3	0.6	1.8	200	500
Net	0.3	2.1	5.9	12.3		
Foreign portfolio investment						
Outward	0.1	3.8	59.7	102.1	3700	2587
Inward	0.3	13.1	16.7	5.4	4267	−59
Net	−0.1	−9.3	43.0	96.7		
International bank lending						
Outward	0.6	2.6	10.6	9.2	333	254
Inward	0.1	−0.2	−0.1	−0.1	. . .	. . .
Net	0.5	2.8	10.7	9.3		
Accumulated external Japanese assets and liabilities						
Assets	na	159.6	437.7	727.3	na	356
Liabilities	na	148.0	307.9	547.0	na	270
Net	13.0[c]	11.6	129.8	180.3		
Comparative information						
GNP ($)	203.1	1040.1	1331.5	1963.2	412	89
GNP (¥ tr.)	73.1	240.1	317.3	330.8	2298	38
World Trade	186.0	1985.0	1922.0	2110.0	967	6
Exchange rates						
¥/$[d]	357.6	226.7	238.5	168.5		
Effective[e]	73.8	100.0	127.1	161.0		

Sources: Bank of Japan, *Economic Statistics Annual*, 1986.
IMF, *International Financial Statistics*, Yearbook 1986 and May 1987.
Daiwa Bank, *Monthly Research Report*, June 1987.
Mitsui & Co., *Mitsui Trade News*, May/June 1987.
GATT, *International Trade*, 1981/1982.
GATT, *Focus*, April 1987.

Notes: a: [(Value 1980 − Value 1970)/Value 1970] × 100. Similarly for 1986/87.
b: CIF values. c: 1973 value. d: Period averages. e: Effective exchange rate against a basket of currencies (based on the IMF's MERM model).

TABLE 8.2 *Japanese internationalisation in a comparative perspective, 1980–1986[a]*
(US$ billions)

| Countries | Net international flows of long-term capital | | | |
	Direct investment	Portfolio investment	Other	Total
Canada	−25.1	35.2	−3.8	6.3
France[b]	−3.0	26.6	−23.2	0.3
Germany	−21.6	48.1	−19.0	7.5
Italy[c]	−3.4	−5.9	24.2	14.9
Japan	−40.1	−152.8	−91.7	−284.6
Netherlands[c]-	−17.3	0.8	−10.8	−27.3
Sweden[c]	−5.8	−4.3	−11.0	−21.1
UK[d]	−22.3	−62.9	−14.4	−99.6
USA	55.3	179.4	−80.2	154.5

Source: IMF, *Balance of Payments Statistics*, May 1987.
Note: a: 1980 to 1986 inclusive. b: Figures for France are up to the 2nd quarter, 1986. c: Figures for Italy, Sweden, Netherlands to 3rd quarter; d: UK to 1st.

TABLE 8.3 *The world's 30 largest banks ranked by assets, 1986 (US$ billions)*

Bank	Assets	Bank	Assets
Dai-Ichi Kangyo	240.74	Sumitomo Trust	125.15
Fuji	213.47	Nat. Westminister	122.86
Sumitomo	206.12	Taiyo Kobe	116.51
Mitsubishi	204.79	Barclays	116.41
Sanwa	192.29	Mitsui Trust	116.05
Citicorp	191.35	Société Générale Long Term Credit	116.01
Industrial Bank of Japan	161.61	Bank of Japan	115.52
Crédit Agricole	154.40	Bank of Tokyo	115.52
Banque Nationale de Paris	141.87	Daiwa	102.83
Tokai	138.45	Bank America Corp.	102.20
Norinchukin	136.92	Yasuda Trust	101.34
Crédit Lyonnais	132.07	Dresdner	101.18
Mitsui	132.04	Chase Manhattan Corp.	94.76
Deutsche	131.80	Union Bank of Switzerland	93.72
Mitsubishi Trust	127.37	Paribas	93.24

Source: *Euromoney*, June 1987.

experience; and (d) the continuing strength of Japan's economy and major commercial institutions. One example of this international prominence is given by Table 8.3, which shows that Japanese banks have edged US and French institutions out of their former pre-eminent positions (as ranked by total assets); the top five banks are Japanese, and they also occupy 17 of the top 30 places.

THE HOLLOW ECONOMY

Yet Japan's internationalisation is not entirely of its own planning, and the government and business community are only too painfully aware of the inherent dangers. Manufacturing firms, in particular, have been driven abroad by the Scylla and Charybdis of increasing low-cost competition from the newly industrialising countries[7] and a dollar in free-fall against the yen:

> Businessmen and government officials, sounding plaintively like their counterparts in the US Rust Belt, stew about the 'hollowing out' of their industries. They have a point. Fully 20% of the country's manufacturing will take place overseas by the turn of the century, vs under 5% today....As a result, manufacturing employment is heading inexorably downwards.[8]

The concept of a 'hollow economy' in which manufacturing plays a minimal role was first introduced by *Business Week*[9] in an analysis of the deindustrialisation of the USA. Japanese companies hope to avoid the pitfalls encountered by their counterparts elsewhere, but the pressure to secure foreign markets (e.g. via massive manufacturing investments in the USA) and reduce costs (by investing in the developing countries of Latin America and Pacific Asia) remains intense. In 1986, over half of the 100 largest Japanese companies[10] saw their sales fall, and a third recorded a decline in profits (albeit only seven of these, mainly in steel and shipbuilding, actually suffered a loss).

Despite the difficulties of the country's domestic manufacturers, foreign companies continued to invest in Japan. The bulk of foreign direct investment in Japan (of which three-quarters in in manufacturing) has arrived since 1980,[11] in effect during a period contemporaneous with Japanese foreign expansion. The annual flow of inward FDI tripled to US$1.8 billion between 1985 and 1986 (Table 8.1), clearly manifesting considerable commitment by foreign companies to the Japanese economy. According to JETRO, as the Japanese economy spreads its wings:

US and European multinational businesses are expanding their investment in Japan (R & D investment also [*sic*]) in such high-tech fields as
electrical machinery, electronics and pharmaceuticals. Investment in the
financial and securities fields is also on the increase.[12]

Given that Japanese manufacturing companies are moving abroad under
intense competitive pressures, are foreign multinationals moving into
calamity? Or is there a method in their madness? This chapter will try to
shed some light on such questions by exploring some of the results of a
continuing study of European companies with a manufacturing presence in
Japan.

SALMO EUROPAR PROFILED

The project referred to above (the 'Bradford Study') has a current sample
size of 28 European parent companies with at least one manufacturing
affiliate in Japan, though many companies have several such affiliates. The
methodology of the research involves the questionnaire-based interview of
executives at each parent company *and* also of executives at their affiliates
in Japan. Information was collected on a great many aspects of European
companies' strategy and experience in Japan,[13, 14] but this chapter will
examine only some of the results.

Table 8.4 gives details of foreign investors in Japan. In total, European
companies comprise only about a fifth of all foreign direct investment in
Japan by value, but their share of annual inward investment is increasing: in
1985, this share was almost a third – and was probably greater in 1986. A
comparison of columns 2 and 3 of Table 8.4 (see table note 'c') indicates
that the 28 parent companies (and 79 affiliates) in the Bradford Study
represent a fair share of European companies with manufacturing bases in
Japan. (The total number of European affiliates established in Japan is of
the order of 1100, but most of these are not involved in manufacturing.)
The firms interviewed were domiciled in nine different West European
countries (seven EC member countries), roughly in proportion to the scale
of each country's manufacturing presence in Japan. The table also shows
that there is a concentration of manufacturing investments in two broad
industrial categories: chemicals and machinery. The firms in the Bradford
Study roughly fit this pattern.

TABLE 8.4 *A profile of foreign investors in Japan*

Country or industry	Total value of inward FDI 1950–85[a] (US$ mill.)	Total no. of manuf. affils, 1972–86[c]	Bradford Study No. of parent companies	Bradford Study No. of affiliates[b]
Belgium	6.8	na	2	4
Denmark	12.3	2	4	5
France	137.5	11	3	15
Germany	250.4	17	4	17
Italy	na	na	2	5
Netherlands	166.4	4	3	9
Sweden	84.9	7	2	10
Switzerland	377.5	12	3	4
UK	318.5	8	5	10
Other Europe	74.0			
USA	3040.6	109		
Other countries	1778.3	7		
Commerce	773.6			
Construction and real estate	41.3			
Transportation/ communications	20.1			
Warehousing	43.5			
Other services	275.8			
Others	526.9			
Manufacturing	4566.1	177	28	79
Ceramics	113.5	4	1	
Chemicals[d]	2162.7	66	14	
Machinery[e]	1447.6	61	11	
Metal products	408.3	10	2	
Textiles	31.4	2		
Petroleum and pet. products	606.2	2		
Rubber	36.7			
Food	157.8	7		
Others	208.0	25		
Total	6247.2	177	28	79

Sources: MITI, Bank of Japan, Bradford Study.
Notes: a: Approvals/notifications. b: All parent companies in the study are involved in manufacturing in Japan, but this does not apply to all of their affiliates. c: Only affiliates with 50 per cent or or more foreign ownership. d: Includes pharmaceuticals. e: Includes all machinery: general, electronic, precision, etc.

STRATEGY BY CONSECUTIVE REASONING[15]

The motivations underlying the 28 parent firms' manufacturing investments in Japan are complex, but despite the heterogeneous nature of the sample (in terms of source country, industry, size), it is possible to establish a general framework of strategic intent. This is perhaps best analysed by discussion in terms of three interrelated sub-categories of strategy:

1. The bottom line

In one form or another, the single most important reason for entering the Japanese market was almost universally the size and potential of the country's market (Table 8.5). Of course, this was frequently qualified by contingent factors, e.g. import barriers, need to expand market share, need to service specific customers, but the primacy of Japan's market remains. The same conclusion, hardly surprising since Japan constitutes over 10 per cent of the world economy, is confirmed in recent surveys by the Nomura Research Institute (Table 8.9, categories 1 and 2) and JETRO.[16]   At this level, the decision to manufacture in Japan is defined largely on the basis of cost: tariff barriers and transportation costs (e.g. for bulky machinery and plant) are positive influences, while global economies of scale (on 'commodity' chemicals) tend to reduce the likelihood of local manufacturing.

However, there is always an element of service provision in the marketing of manufactured goods, and the need to tailor products to the specific tastes and requirements (indeed whims) of Japanese customers was frequently sufficient justification for establishing a manufacturing base.

TABLE 8.5 *The single most important reason leading to manufacturing investment in Japan*

Reason	Number of parents
1. Japanese market size, rate of growth, or potential[a]	15
2. To cover world market	8
3. To control marketing efforts in Japan	2
4. Defensive reasons	2
5. Technological reasons	1
Total	28

Source: Bradford Study.
Note: a: Includes difficulty of market access due to barriers, etc.

TABLE 8.6 *The target market of European investors in Japan*

Category	Number of parents
1. Industrial customers only	12
2. A range of customers[a]	11
3. Not known	5
Total	28

Source: Bradford Study.
Note: a: Of which three or four companies are almost entirely consumer-market oriented.

One interesting finding of the Bradford Study is that about half of the sample companies are orientated solely towards industrial customers (Table 8.6). Three factors jointly explain this bias: the highly competitive Japanese market permits only firms with advanced technological expertise or other advantages to survive; industrial customers are easier to locate (especially given the complex distribution system), and these customers are demanding in regard to specifications and quality. The last point tends to enforce a Japanese presence.

Another factor is that the firms in the Bradford Study tend to take a long-term view. The potential rewards of the Japanese market are deemed to be sufficiently great to justify low profits while the affiliates are (or were) establishing a firm local foothold. Japan's current difficulties are seen to be short-term ones of readjustment, while the potentialities of Japanese liberalisation are seen as immense.[17]

TABLE 8.7 *'Reverse' transfer of technology and expertise*

'Does your presence in the Japanese market stimulate the home company to make better or more competitive products?'[a]	Number of parents
Yes	15
Not yet, but expected to	5
No	6
Not known	2
Total	28

Source: Bradford Study.
Note: a: For example, through technology or skill transfer

2. Presence effects and the insider

Though the size of the Japanese market is sufficient to warrant attention and some cost and service considerations may determine the establishment of local manufacturing facilities, these factors do not explain the full range and extent of manufacturing FDI in Japan. The Bradford Study suggests that much of the explanation for this FDI lies in the considerable externalities obtained from a presence in Japan.

(a) Presence effects. One way of looking at these effects is by dividing the barriers to trading in Japan into three types. The first type is simply tariff (and similar) barriers which can be surmounted by jumping the tariff wall, as discussed above, or making an impact at inter-governmental and international fora. A second type is non-tariff measures (NTMs), which are introduced by national authorities or business organisations (e.g. standards and specifications, both mandatory and voluntary) and are either complied with (as many in the sample chose, sometimes to their advantage) or countered with a great deal of fuss. The fact that companies can exploit NTMs to their benefit may warrant a local investment. Finally, there are non-tariff barriers other than NTMs (NTBs) which, in the case of Japan, include language and culture; patriotism and a degree of xenophobia; and distinctive business ethics. According to the sample of firms in the Bradford Study, a local presence was frequently beneficial in such cases. For example, customers are more willing to purchase goods from European firms producing in Japan because such firms are regarded as being near-Japanese; better qualified personnel are more willing to work for foreign firms with a track record of commitment to the Japanese economy (a recent study lends credence to this view);[18] and a local presence is a considerable boon for establishing links with Japanese firms; relationships are long-term and between friends.

(b) Learning effects. Most firms believed that their manufacturing

TABLE 8.8 *European views on relative productivity performance*

'Japanese productivity is':	*Number of parents*
Higher than European productivity	11
The same as European productivity	5
Lower than European productivity	4
Don't know	8
Total	28

Source: Bradford Study.

presence in the Japanese economy helped them to produce better products (Table 8.7), though some argued that such benefits were not uncommon in other markets. Some firms designed better products simply because of the adaptations to production methods dictated by the exacting requirements (especially in quality) of Japanese customers. Others said that they had learned from Japanese production methods *per se*, often in factories run with Japanese joint venture partners,[19] and the skills/techniques most frequently cited as acquired were better quality and inventory control. It was also the view of most firms that Japanese productivity performance was higher than that in Europe, but this was usually qualified by the point that 'productivity' was not the right term for comparison purposes. The output per person may be higher, but only because Japanese employees continue work until they complete a task, often unpaid[20] (Table 8.8).

(c) Insider benefits. There are considerable benefits to be gained by being considered part of the Japanese domestic scene. Few European investors could claim to be anywhere close to such an exalted position, but local production is considered an essential credential. At the fringes, some firms

TABLE 8.9 *US and European companies' motivations underlying the establishment of new bases or expansion of existing bases (Non-financial companies only)*

Reasons given (multiple responses included)	Number			%		
	USA (A)	Europe (B)	Total (C)	USA (A/D)	Europe (B/D)	Total (C/D)
Market						
1. The scale and growth prospects of East Asia/Pacific Basin market	32	45	78	52.5	62.5	58.2
2. The scale and growth prospects of the Japanese market in particular	44	50	95	72.1	69.4	70.9
Industrial, corporate						
3. The presence of many multinationals	6	5	12	9.8	6.9	9.0
4. Rival corporations have already entered Japan	9	8	18	14.8	11.1	13.4

continued on next page

Table 8.9 contd.

5. Many of the affiliated group corporations have already entered Japan	1	4	5	1.6	5.6	3.7
6. The presence of good candidates for joint venture partners	27	39	67	44.3	54.2	50.0
7. The presence of suppliers of quality components	10	16	26	16.4	22.2	19.4
Business resources						
8. Ample supply of quality labour	5	8	13	8.2	11.1	9.7
9. Concentration of information (on Asian market, advanced technology, etc.)	15	28	44	24.6	38.9	32.8
10. Availability of sophisticated technology	9	26	36	14.8	36.1	26.9
11. Ready capital procurement	8	10	19	13.1	13.9	14.2
Conditions						
12. Political, economic, and social stability	33	33	67	54.1	45.8	50.0
13. Preferential treatment in the context of industrial policy	2	3	5	3.3	4.2	5.7
14. Hedge against exchange risks	4	7	11	6.6	9.7	8.2
15. Transportation and communication centre of East Asia/ Pacific Basin	17	18	36	27.9	25.0	26.9
16. Surmount export barriers to Japan	16	24	40	26.2	33.3	29.9
17. Other	6	1	7	9.8	1.4	5.2
Total number of firms (D)	61	72	134			

Source: Nomura Research Institute's 1986 study of companies with an inclination to enter Japan.

are beginning to be accepted as members of Japanese corporate associations, while others are making use of cheap Japanese finance in their international operations. Many firms referred to Japan as an 'information paradise' and are able to use information gained in Japan throughout the globe. The Nomura study (Table 8.9) confirms the importance of information: 28 out of 72 European firms refer to this as a reason for their considering investment/expansion in Japan.

(d) The potential of the re-structured Japan. There is little doubt (except in Japan!) that Japanese companies will emerge from their current plight as formidable competitors:

> The factories that remain could be world-beaters. Japanese companies are slashing costs and diversifying aggressively into advanced, premium-priced products and are pouring money into better manufacturing techniques. Some of the biggest exporters have slimmed down enough to operate profitably at 140 yen to the dollar. Toyota Motor Corp., for example, is said to be cutting the time it takes to bore engine blocks from 1 minute to 30 seconds....Japanese business spending on civilian R & D as a percentage of the economy remains significantly larger than that of the US and the gap is widening.[21]

Many of the advanced technologies of the future will be developed in Japan, particularly in the information-related industries (Table 8.10). Though the Bradford Study did not address this question directly, it is clear from the responses of executives in both Europe and Japan that a local manufacturing and R & D presence was regarded as essential for future competitiveness – and even survival – since this enabled Europeans to remain near (if not in) the forefront of new technological developments. This view is also clear from the Nomura research (Table 8.9, category10).

3. The strategic long run

A number of commentators, including Ohmae,[22] have recently argued that rapid technological change, increased competitiveness, and escalating production costs are forcing international companies into new strategic decisions. On the one hand, firms are increasingly stressing a presence in the three major loci of the industrialised world (Europe, Japan, and the USA) in order to ensure security of supply and market (and exchange threat with other major companies), and, on the other hand, it is suggested that firms increasingly establish collaborative agreements to reduce costs and mutual risks.[23]

TABLE 8.10 *MITI information technology development projects*

Project name	Description, elements working name	Budget (¥ billion), duration
Material and device technology		
New functional devices	Three–dimensional integrated circuits, super lattice devices, biodevices	7.8 (FY 1981–86)
High-speed science and technology computation system	Very high–speed devices	23.0 (FY 1981–89)
Optoelectronic integrated circuits	OEIC	10.0 (FY 1985–95)
Applied synchrotron radiation technology	SOR (X-ray lithography)	14.3 (FY 1985–95)
Information processing technology		
Fifth-generation computer project	Artificial intelligence, natural language processing, machine translation, man–machine interface	About 20.0 FY 1986 (FY 1982–91)
Software technology development	Technology to integrate software environment	(1982–)
High-speed science and technology computing system*	High-speed processing, large-capacity high-speed memory, decentralised processing machines, other	23.0 (FY 1981–89)
Data-base system for mutual computer operation	Multimedia, decentralised data base, other	15.0 (FY 1985–91)
Machine translation system with neighbouring countries	Machine translation	6.25 (FY1986–92)
Electronic dictionary for processing natural languages	Fifth–generation computer language concept and knowledge base	Minimum 14.3 (FY 1985–94)
Industrial software production system	Sigma project	25.0 (FY 1985–94)
Telecommunications technology		
Data-base system for computer inter-operability*	Data transmission software, promotion of OSI, establishment of inter-operability conformity	15.0 (FY 1985–91)

continued on next page

Table 8.10 contd.

Project name	Description	Budget (duration)
Basic measuring technology for coherent optical communications	Laser technology, high-efficiency, high-density, high–modulation system	4.3 (FY 1985–91)
Space technology		
Resources exploration observation system	Composite open radar, engineering sensor, high-speed, large-capacity transfer technology	23.0 (FY 1984–90)
Utilisation of space observation	Develop space-environment testing device	5.7 (FY 1985–92)
Application systems		
Medical treatment support system	MEDIS	Undecided (FY 1982–88)
Robots for hazardous tasks	Image recognition, other	20.0 (FY 1983–90)
Advanced information processing-type image information system	Advanced HI-OVIS	4.8 (FY 1985–90)
Commissioned R&D on medical and welfare equipment	CT scanner, nervous disorder diagnosis, medical treatment support system	(FY 1976–)
Electrotechnical laboratory projects		
Materials	Electronic material, magnetic and amorphous materials, other	
Electronic devices	High-speed devices, new functional devices, other	
Pattern information	Voice, image recognition, bionics, other	
Computers	Information processing, storage, input-output technology, other	
Software	Program lanuage, network architecture, other	
Control	Information system control technology, other	
Microwave and electronics	Laser, optoelectronics technology, other	
Information technology in extreme environments	Space environment technology, other	

Source: Seiji Hagiwara, 'Creating Tomorrow's Information Technology', *Journal of Japanese Trade & Industry*, No. 3, 1987.
Note: *Items straddle technological fields.

TABLE 8.11 *Sales in Japan as a share of European firm's global sales*

Share	Number of parents
Up to 2%	3
2–4%	7
5–10%	11
11–15%	2
Over 15%	1
Not known	4
Total	28

Source: Bradford Study.

TABLE 8.12 *Ownership arrangements of the affiliates of European manufacturing investors in Japan*

Arrangement	Number of affiliates
100% European participation[a]	22
Majority European participation	10
50:50 European-Japanese participation	30
Minority European participation	9
Not known	8
Total	79

Source: Bradford Study.
Note: a: Not necessarily a single European parent company.

The Bradford study does provide some support for these hypotheses. Table 8.11 shows the present share of Japan in the global networks of the sample firms. Most firms were of the opinion that their share of the Japanese market had to be expanded. This view was frequently expressed in terms of a 'triangular concept' of the world market, which necessitated having a manufacturing presence in the three major power bases of the world economy, Europe, Japan, and the USA (see also the second category of Table 8.5).[24] In a world economy in crisis, with the possibility of increased protectionism and a division of the globe into 'blocs', such an insider role has considerable merit.

In terms of collaboration between European investors and Japanese firms, the results of the study are more mixed. As Table 8.12 shows, most affiliates in Japan are joint ventures, and this tendency is also apparent from

Table 8.9 (category 6). However, this preference for joint ventures is more readily explained in terms of their facilitating rapid access into a market which is difficult to penetrate. Having said this, a number of 'world-scale' companies in the sample are clearly establishing close collaborative links with Japanese counterparts, links involving joint production, joint research, cross-licensing, and a variety of other forms. These and other firms, nevertheless, remained cautious; after all, the Japanese *keiretsu* have a century of experience in inter-company collaboration! But a recent publication by JETRO identifies a large number of Euro-Japanese collaborative agreements of various types.[25]

CONCLUDING REMARKS

Most executives regarded their manufacturing presence in Japan as successful (Table 8.13), but this opinion was normally expressed in terms of success (i) in comparison with other foreign competitors or (ii) relative to their modest objectives in a market that requires long-term commitment. In general, this commitment was secure, though some affiliates were concerned regarding the attitude of their European parents. The most abiding impression emerging from the Bradford Study is that a base in the Japanese economy is frequently viewed as being strategically crucial, especially since the reshaped Japan of the future will be even more competitive than today. However, caution is also a key word, since Japan is a difficult market to enter and, moreover, there are lucrative opportunities elsewhere in the world economy. Nevertheless, apart from the 'nuts and bolts' reasons for manufacturing locally, strategic necessity makes an insider presence in Japan absolutely vital for many firms.

TABLE 8.13 *The perception of success in Japan at the European headquarters*

	Number of parents
Very successful	12
Successful	8
Satisfied, but more can be achieved	7
Unsuccessful	1
Total	28

Source: Bradford Study.

Notes

1. With apologies to John Wyndham.
2. See 'Takeover Artists Learn the Moves', *Business Week*, 3 August 1987, p. 16.
3. See Seiichi Tsukazaki, 'Japanese Direct Investment Abroad', *Journal of Japanese Trade and Industry*, No. 4, 1987.
4. See Daiwa Bank, *Monthly Research Report*, June 1988.
5. Frequently the investment is to the USA.
6. Table 8.2 is highly aggregated, but even when the figures are disaggregated, Japan is still far ahead.
7. Indeed, the low-cost competition could be from anywhere – including Europe.
8. 'Fear and Trembling in the Colossus', *Fortune*, 30 March 1987, p. 32.
9. 'The Hollow Corporation', *Business Week*, 3 March 1986.
10. *Business Week*, 3 July 1987.
11. The year 1980 saw the full liberalisation of the regime controlling the inflow of foreign direct investment.
12. JETRO, *White Paper on World and Japanese Overseas Direct Investment (summary)*, Tokyo, February 1987.
13. The questionnaire was 16 pages long.
14. Peter J. Buckley, Hafiz Mirza, and John R. Sparkes, *Success in Japan: How European Firms Compete in the Japanese Market* (Oxford: Basil Blackwell, 1988). There have been a number of reports and articles on other aspects of the Bradford Study. These include *European Affiliates in Japan*, a report submitted to the Japan Foundation, 1984; 'Key to successful investment by foreign companies', *Investors Chronicle*, 19, September 1986; 'A note on Japanese pricing policy', *Applied Economics*, Vol. 19, no. 6; and 'Direct Foreign Investment in Japan as a means of market entry: the case of European firms', *Journal of Marketing Management*, Vol. 2, no. 3, 1987. In addition, there has also been a more specific study of British firms based on a postal questionnaire: *British Companies' Investments in Japan*, report submitted to the Great Britain–Sasakawa Foundation, 1987.
15. With apologies to John Keats.
16. JETRO, op. cit., page 6.
17. See 'Dismantling the Barriers in Tokyo', *Banker*, June 1987.
18. See The Institute for International Business Communication, *Foreign Affiliates in Japan: The Search for Professional Manpower*, Tokyo, 1987.
19. It is not uncommon to find the manufacturing production taking place on the existing site of the Japanese joint venture partner.
20. But many executives did note the superior talents of a Japanese team working together.
21. 'Remaking Japan', *Business Week*, 13 July 1987, p. 39.
22. Kenichi Ohmae, *Triad Power: The Coming Shape of Global Competition* (New York: Free Press, 1985).
23. On cooperation between firms, see Peter J. Buckley and Mark Casson, 'A Theory of Cooperation in International Business', *Management International Review* (forthcoming) and F. J. Contractor and P. Lorange (eds.), *Cooperative Strategies in International Business* (Lexington, Mass.: Lexington Books; London: D.C. Heath & Co. 1987).

24.   Many executives took a wider definition of the 'Japan' part of the triangle, frequently including Korea, Taiwan, and other parts of Pacific Asia.

25.   JETRO, *Cooperations Between European and Japanese Firms: Cases of Industrial Collaboration*, Tokyo, 1986.

9 New Multinationals for Old? The Political Economy of Japanese Internationalisation

Hafiz Mirza, Peter J. Buckley and John R. Sparkes

1. *LE DÉFI JAPONAIS?*

In the 1960s researchers suddenly discovered the multinational company (especially the American variety, apparently in the process of engulfing Europe, if not the rest of the world) and all its works. Many sang the praises of its prowess and technological achievements, though others stressed the various problems associated with its operations. The latter view was, perhaps, more prevalent during the 1970s; but the former persuasion has increasingly gained credence in recent years as nations, struggling against the blight of economic turmoil, have turned (often with indecent haste) to multinational companies for salvation.

None of these views or attitudes is entirely correct. Capitalism has been international since its inception and the 'modern' multinational company has had numerous illustrious forebears. Moreover, the multinational company (MNC), as international capitalism in microcosm, contains within it both the seeds of progress and the potential for a grim harvest. Given their international spread, issues of concern can be examined from a variety of perspectives: international production and trade has implications for source countries (is employment at home reduced, are foreign markets gained?), host countries (are there technological gains, increased dependence?) and the international community (does increased interdependence increase economic and financial volatility?).

For many years Japan avoided these issues by restricting inward and outward direct investment by multinational companies. Outward direct investment was not liberalised until the early 1970s, while foreign multinationals had to wait until the 1980s before they could make substantial inroads into the Japanese economy. More recently, however, these issues have come to the fore because of rapid outward and inward international investment. For example, given the current rate of outward FDI, it is feasible that international production by Japanese multinationals will be the equivalent of 10 per cent of Japanese GNP by the mid-1990s. In current terms this is equal to about US$240bn, larger than either the Spanish or Dutch economies; and about half the size of the UK's GNP. Of the developing countries, only China's GNP exceeds this amount; and neither the ASEAN countries nor East Asian NICs (taken as a whole) quite measure up to this scale.

Of course, Japanese multinationals will not be alone in their global activities (those from the USA, the UK, Germany, France and the Netherlands are of especial importance), but the consequences of their internationalisation need some scrutiny and are the subject of this chapter.

2. SOME PERSPECTIVES ON JAPANESE INTERNATIONALISATION

It is clear that Japanese internationalisation is fundamentally a consequence of the country's postwar development and emergence as the world's second largest economy. On most measures Japan is less 'internationalised' than other equivalent countries; and the global expansion of the country's major companies can be viewed simply as a 'catching-up' exercise. Japanese companies today rank with the world's largest and, not unexpectedly, seek business in all quarters of the world. As a consequence, the last few years have seen a huge surge in Japan's net international assets (according to the Japanese Ministry of Finance these rose from a few billion dollars to nearly US$250 billion in 1987). This surge reflects the better performance of the Japanese economy (compared to its international competitors), the domestic difficulties created by the consequent rise in the value of the yen (the speed of the yen's ascent has also been fuelled by a collapse of confidence in the dollar) – and the sheer fact that an ascendant yen reduces the cost of outward foreign investment.

The contours of Japanese internationalisation are such that visible trade, invisible trade, foreign direct investment, foreign portfolio investment and international bank lending have all expanded rapidly at various times (chronologically, roughly in the order given); but it is probably fair to argue that the *relative* expansion of each of these elements has essentially been balanced.

Table 9.1 summarises the spread of these international activities in 1988. It is important to note that Japan has a perennial surplus in only the balance of visible trade; in all other items, the country has been running a deficit for

TABLE 9.1 *Japan's net balance of payments by item, country and country groups, 1988 (US$ billions)*

Item	USA	UK	EC	Other OECD	LDCs	World
Visible trade	54.9	3.7	18.0	3.4	9.6	92.8
Invisible trade	–0.6	–2.2	–3.1	–0.1	–3.3	–4.9
Of which:						
* Tourism	–2.1	–0.4	–1.2	–0.5	–1.7	–5.8
* Investment income	3.2	–0.7	0.3	1.2	2.1	9.5
Direct investment	–7.8	–1.0	–2.7	–0.6	–3.0	–14.3
Portfolio investment	–55.9	0.6	–29.0	–6.2	–6.5	–101.5
International bank loans	–0.7	0.0	–1.0	–2.3	–5.2	–9.3
Other items	–1.7	–1.2	–1.6	–0.3	–2.4	–8.8
Basic Balance	–11.9	neg	–19.5	–6.3	–10.7	–45.6

Source: Buckley, Mirza and Witt (1989)

the last few years. However, apart from invisibles, the other deficits are hardly problematic since they ensure large-scale overseas holdings of income-generating assets. This fact is reflected in a rising net investment income which offsets the deficit in invisible trade. The rest of the world enjoys a surplus in 'tourism', but this could also be a worrying trend.[1] The country's major international partner is obviously the USA, but a number of European Community and developing countries are also important (as section 4 will reveal).

The *endaka-fukyo* (high yen recession) induced by the considerable and rapid appreciation of the yen has forced a wholescale restructuring of the Japanese economy. However, despite the fears regarding the 'hollow' economy, the country has emerged stronger than ever. One of the reasons for this is that the strong yen had positive as well as negative consequences, chiefly because of a fall in the cost of imports. The implications of this restructuring are further discussed in sections 3 and 4.

3. JAPANESE INTERNATIONALISATION AND THE INDUSTRIALISED COUNTRIES

Much of Japan's internationalisation has been spurred on by attempts to reduce its trade surplus. This issue looms large in many industrialised countries, especially in the USA and a number of EC states. However, many commentators have argued that the crucial issue is actually over jobs and that 'Western' multinationals are as guilty as Japanese companies in ensuring that production and jobs have hitherto been retained in Japan through inward direct investment and licensing.[2]

This point becomes clear if we recognise that companies have three broad ways of servicing foreign markets: exporting, overseas production and licensing. If a US company were to choose to export to Japan, then production (and hence jobs) would be in the USA; if production in Japan was chosen, the US company would obviously employ *Japanese workers*; if licensing was chosen as the main route (and theoretically this is best since an income – royalties – is received with few resources expended) then a *Japanese company* would employ *Japanese workers*. Bearing these options in mind, it is clear from Figure 9.1 that US and Japanese companies sold about the same number of goods in each others' markets in the mid-1980s.

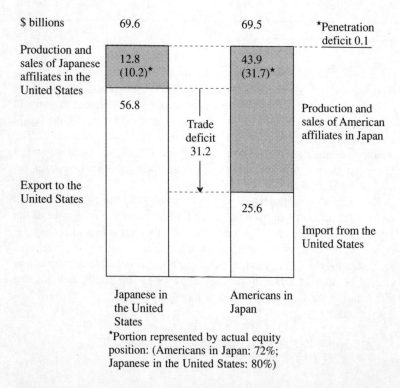

FIGURE 9.1 *Presence of USA and Japanese companies in each others' markets, 1984*

Source: Kenichi Ohmae (1987)

(They are equally 'interpenetrated'.) However, American companies prefer to produce most of the goods they sell in the Japanese marketplace in Japan itself (factors such as comparative advantage, the quality of labour, the need to tailor products to local requirements can be used to explain this tendency): hence Japanese workers are used in preference to US employees and this jobs-gap is reflected in the USA's trade deficit (though exporting from the USA is unlikely to 'repatriate' all these jobs to North America). If licensing is brought into the picture the USA has an 'interpenetration surplus' with Japan since the latter is a net importer of technology – but, though the USA receives an income from these technology exports, the jobs go to Japanese workers in Japanese companies. This analysis also applies to Japan's relations with other industrialised countries, albeit to a lesser extent.

Japanese internationalisation, particularly because of the yen appreciation following the G-7 accords and the consequent decline in Japanese competitiveness, is thus partly a way of reducing the trade surplus and exporting jobs. The indications are that this is not occurring to the extent expected and that other problems are arising. Sticking to the US–Japan trade/job problem, it is clear that, though a large number of Japanese companies have expanded production in the USA (and employ many more local workers), a number of common host country worries are emerging: are the jobs in advanced technologies, is there increased dependence on Japan, should there be local content requirements, how good are linkages with US companies? (There are also, of course, a number of hopes for a transfer of more effective management, quality control, etc. to the USA and other host economies.) In addition the large-scale acquisition of US business and property by Japan (and other countries, especially the UK) is raising the spectre of a USA beholden to foreign interests – and there are increasing demands for control of inward foreign investment, particularly by screening out unwelcome projects and bids.

Another issue is that the trade/jobs gap with Japan has been replaced with that from another source: many Japanese companies have preferred to transfer production to developing countries in East Asia or South America and export from there. This strategy both dodges the yen appreciation and makes production more competitive because of cheap local labour costs. A final point is that Japan has managed to restructure much more effectively than was expected and competitiveness has not always declined drastically. Table 9.2 shows how quickly Japanese manufacturers have cut costs in the wake of the yen appreciation: though some companies will inevitably succumb, many remain competitive internationally, albeit with lower profit margins. This adaptation has been possible for three reasons: (i) cheaper import prices, especially for raw materials; (ii) increased sourcing of components from abroad, taking advantage of the yen's strength and cheap

TABLE 9.2 *Break-even rates of Japanese industries (yen/dollar)*

	Apr.–Sept. 1985 (a)	Apr.–Sept. 1986	Apr–Sept 1987	Oct. 1987– Mar. 1988 (b)	(b–a)
Total (1)	210	152	131	114	–96
General machinery	204	148	127	101	–103
Electrical machinery	203	148	126	109	–94
Transportation machinery	216	155	133	118	–98
Precision machinery	216	155	137	120	–96
Exchange rate (period average) (2)	245	163	145	132	–133
(2)–(1)	+35	+11	+14	+18	–

Note: Break-even rates are calculated as follows:
Given ordinary profit equalling domestic sales plus export sales (dollar-denominated exports value × exchange rate) minus expenses (raw materials and energy, staff, financial, etc, the exchange rate at which ordinary profit would be reduced to zero can be called the break-even rate.

Source: Industrial Bank of Japan, *Quarterly Survey of Japanese Finance and Industry*, No 74, 1988.

labour/input costs in East Asia; and (iii) rationalisation of production and introduction of new technology. There were few doubts that Japan would adapt, but the speed has surprised many analysts.

Table 9.3 shows how well the Japanese economy has performed (and is expected to perform), despite the difficult circumstances. One of the problems for the USA and other industrialised economies is that foreign companies are increasingly investing in Japan (the 1987 inflow of US$2.5 billion was a fourfold increase over 1985) and though the amounts are small compared to outward Japanese direct investment, the jobs/trade balance issue identified earlier could well remain prominent – especially if inward FDI continues to increase. From the point of view of the foreign investors, of course, a local presence is essential for effective market servicing. This contradiction (i.e. US and European MNCs play a role in producing Japan's trade surplus with their source countries) is yet another example of the fact that the interests of multinationals and nation-states may not ultimately coincide.

TABLE 9.3 *The Japanese economy of the late 1980s compared with selected major industrialised countries*

Item	Japan	USA	Germany	UK
A. 1987 GNP (US$ bn)	2 384.5	4 488.6	1 125.6	678.9
B. 1987 GNP/capita (US$)	19 500	18 500	18 500	11 900
C. Real GDP/GNP growth Rate (%)				
1982–86 average	3.7	2.8	1.7	2.6
1987 outturn	4.2	3.4	1.7	3.3
1988 forecast	5.2	4.0	2.2	3.2
1989 forecast	4.0	2.5	1.7	2.0
D. Gross Fixed Capital Formation (% of GNP)				
1980–87 average	29.0	18.1	20.5	16.7
E. Unemployment Rate (% of workforce, June 1988)	3.0	6.0	7.9	10.4
F. Short Term Interest Rates (%), August 1988	4.0	7.0	5.0	12.0
G. Inflation Rate (%)				
1980–86 average	1.9	3.8	2.6	5.5
1987 outturn	0.1	3.7	0.3	4.1
1988 forecast	0.7	4.2	1.3	4.6
1989 forecast	2.5	1.8	5.0	4.8
H. Change in Unit Labour Costs (%), 1985–87.				
Own Currency	–1.8	–1.2	3.3	3.1
In US$	26.1	–1.2	31.8	15.9
I. Balance of Payments, 1987 (US$ bn)				
Trade Balance	96.4	–159.2	68.6	–15.9
Invisibles Balance	–9.4	–1.5	–23.5	12.9
Current Account Balance	87.0	160.7	45.1	–3.0
Current Account Forecast				
1988	75.0	–145.0	40.0	–21.0
1989	70.0	40.0	–120.0	–26.0
J. 1987 International Bank Assets (US$ bn)	1 552	648	348	254

Sources: Bank for International Settlements, *Annual Report*, June 1988; Barclays Report, August 1988; Morgan Guaranty Trust, *World Financial Markets*, No 4, 1988; *IMF Survey*, 15 and 29 August 1988.

The question of how best to control/influence multinationals will be increasingly raised by industrialised countries (including Japan) over the next few years. A few key issues relevant to Japanese internationalisation include:

(i) The regulation of international banking and portfolio investment. By the end of 1987 the net size of the international banking market was US$2377 billion; US$177 billions of international bonds were issued in 1987; and US$123 billion of international bank credits extended during the same year.[3] The international debt crisis and the October 1987 crash have together increased awareness of the need to regulate the excessive volatility of capital markets. Japan is the foremost player here since it is now the world's largest source of financial and portfolio capital (a consequence of trade surpluses and a high rate of domestic savings).

(ii) The solution of the USA's twin deficits. Japan is effectively financing both of these by building up dollar assets (due to the trade surplus) and purchasing government securities (which have financed the budget deficit). No matter what route is taken to reduce these deficits and relaunch the US economy, Japan is inevitably involved. If the USA goes down a protectionist route, the question whether Japan would pull any strings arises.

(iii) The avoidance of 'techno-nationalism'. One aspect of the protectionist tendency evident in the USA and the EC is the belief that Japan is very willing to acquire the fruits of foreign research, but reluctant to allow access to its own developments. There may be some truth in this, but a structural difference between research is of significance: proportionally more Japanese R&D is conducted by the corporate sector. Not unexpectedly, these companies are reluctant to share their knowledge; but research in universities in the UK and elsewhere is more readily accessible. Since competitiveness in advanced industrial societies is largely technology-driven, this issue will continue to be of considerable importance. Technological developments may become increasingly protected and cross-licensing of research is likely to become a more prominent way of 'servicing' foreign markets, thus leading to an advanced form of cartelisation. Japanese companies can be expected to play a full part in these and other strategic alliances.

(iv) The penetration of political-economic blocs. With the establishment of the single European market in 1992, some protectionist tendencies in the USA, various attempts at establishing 'common markets' in developing countries and the opening-up of the East European and Chinese markets, the appropriate market-servicing strategy becomes increasingly important. Cross-licensing has already been mentioned, but foreign direct investment in the target market is likely to remain of considerable importance to

Japanese multinationals. Significant investments have recently been made in the EC and these are likely to increase. Reciprocity demands can also be expected to increase from all quarters, though these are likely to intensify the regulation of trade, rather than reduce protectionism.

4. JAPANESE INTERNATIONALISATION AND THE DEVELOPING COUNTRIES

In 1987, in consultation with the World Bank, Japan agreed to increase its untied aid to developing countries. US$10 billion dollars were made directly available to the World Bank, the IMF, the Asian Development Bank, etc. for a variety of special funds. A further US$20 billion are to be recycled during 1987–1990 *via* the Asian Development Bank, the Inter-American Development Bank, the Export–Import Bank of Japan and various co-financing organisations. In addition, Japan's official development assistance has increased dramatically in recent years, making it the second largest donor after the USA – and due to overtake the latter by the end of the decade. By 1995 Japan could become the largest single shareholder in the World Bank.[4] This generosity, when many other industrialised countries are reducing their aid, is to be commended, but it is true that much of the aid is likely to go into infrastructural development – in anticipation of increasing foreign direct investment from Japan.

Table 9.4 shows the extent to which Japanese companies, responding to the yen appreciation, have moved their operations to East Asian countries.

TABLE 9.4 *Japan's foreign direct investment in some Asian countries ($m)*

	1985		1986		1987	
	cases	*value*	*cases*	*value*	*cases*	*value*
Hong Kong	105	131	163	50	261	1072
Indonesia	62	408	46	250	67	545
Malaysia	60	79	70	158	64	163
Philippines	9	61	9	21	18	72
Singapore	110	339	85	302	182	494
South Korea	75	134	111	436	166	647
Taiwan	68	114	178	291	268	367
Thailand	51	48	58	124	192	250
Total	540	1314	720	1632	1218	3610

Source: Ministry of Finance (Figures are notifications, not actual flows).

In addition, subcontracting arrangements have been negotiated with many indigenous companies. Sony is a good example of these trends. In 1986 the company had only two significant subsidiaries in Asia: one in Singapore and one in Hong Kong. There are now four new affiliates in Singapore, Malaysia and Thailand producing a significant slice of the company's global output.[5] This expansion will certainly reduce Sony's costs and increase its competitiveness, while expanding jobs and possibly boosting technology transfer to host countries. Should a thousand Sonys bloom? Recipient countries have an ambivalent view of the matter.

Table 9.5 shows the underlying problem from the viewpoint of the NICs and proto-NICs (e.g. Thailand and Malaysia) which are receiving Japanese foreign direct investment. Though Japan has a continuing deficit with raw materials exporters such as Indonesia, Malaysia and China, it has trade surpluses with the NICs, despite increasing its import of manufactures and semi-processed goods in the wake of the yen appreciation. The overall net flow of trade between Asian economies and key Western countries is in Japan's favour. Though Japan has a trade deficit with ASEAN and China because of raw material imports, it retains trade surpluses with most indus-trialised and East Asian countries. The NICs serve as sourcing centres for components and semi-processed goods, but also act as 'aircraft carriers' for

TABLE 9.5 *The geographical distribution of Japan's trade balance, 1980–87 $US billions*

Area or country	Visible trade balance		
	1980	*1986*	*1987*
World	−10.9	83.1	80.3
Industrialised countries of which:	12.9	71.4	72.4
USA	7.3	52.5	53.0
EC	9.8	16.9	20.4
USSR	0.9	1.2	0.2
Developing countries of which:	−28.0	8.2	3.0
Asian NICs[a]	4.0	14.5	16.3
ASEAN[b]	−13.8	−10.5	−8.1
Middle East	−30.4	−20.6	−11.6
South America	2.8	2.3	1.8

Source: IFM, *Direction of Trade Statistics*, 1988 Yearbook.
          a: Korea, Hong Kong and Singapore only. b: Excludes Singapore.

Japanese companies servicing markets in North America, Europe and elsewhere. Some indigenous companies may be independent, but also depend on Japan for licensed technology. In January–October 1987, Korean companies paid Japanese and US licensors US$154 million and US$163 million respectively in royalty fees, about 80 per cent of total royalty payments. Royalty payments to Japanese companies have climbed steadily relative to US firms and are soon expected to occupy the top spot.

East Asian countries are fully aware of the dangers of Japanese domination (this is why the 'Pacific Economic Community' remains a vision); and argue strenuously against any notion of a 'stratified Asian division of labour' in which the NICs relinquish textiles to the ASEAN nations, receiving in turn steel, shipbuilding, perhaps consumer electronics from Japan. Most East Asian countries have their sights on a high-tech future and such a division of labour is antithetical to this aspiration. Nevertheless, Japan is the regional superpower with a GNP far larger than all East Asian countries put together. Economic necessity is forcing the establishment (or further entrenchment) of a division of labour in the region which is likely to create much resentment. Japan should pay considerable heed to the views of its neighbours on issues such as technology transfer, employment, local sensibilities, etc. Two other issues regarding Japanese internationalisation are important in this respect. First, in common with other multinationals, Japanese companies are likely to create many difficulties for the development process and local cultures. This can only be avoided on the basis of close cooperation with host governments and groups representing the local populations. Secondly, by expanding further in East Asia and South America, Japanese multinationals are more likely to come into competition with indigenous and foreign multinationals already well established in developing countries (especially in growing markets such as Pacific Asia). This has implications for strategy, but from the point of view of developing country populations, the likely consequences of this competition lend weight to the old Indian proverb 'whether elephants make war or love, grass suffers'.

5. CONCLUDING REMARKS

The relationship between Japan's growing economic strength and its political quiescence since the end of the Second World War continues to be a source of speculation. Pressure is put on this relationship by rapid progress and the internationalisation of the Japanese economy. It is, for instance, suggested that perhaps 3 to 5 per cent of Japan's national wealth will be generated in a few Pacific Asian countries by the turn of the century. Should reaction to

Japanese inward foreign investment become adverse, then Japanese multinationals will be tempted to turn to their government for protection, as multinational have done in other countries. However, all the indications are that any pressure for direct action will be resisted (as it was, for instance, in the Gulf crisis precipitated by Iraq's annexation of Kuwait). More subtle forms of persuasion are likely to be employed against host nations which threaten Japanese subsidiaries.

Notes

1. Peter J. Buckley, Halfiz Mirza and Stephen F. Witt, 'Japan's International Tourism in the Context of its International Economic Relations,' *Service Industries Journal* Vol. 9, no. 3, July 1989.
2. Kenichi Ohmae, 'Companies without Countries,' *The McKinsey Quarterly*, Autumn 1987.
3. *World Financial Markets*, Issue 4, 1988.
4. *South*, September 1988.
5. *Far Eastern Economic Review*, 16 June 1988.
6. *Korea Trade and Business*, February 1988.

Index

Penrose, Edith T. 71, 81n
performance 21-2
  budgeting 14
Pfeffer, Jeffrey 9, 12n, 63
pharmaceuticals 95
Philippines 157-8
Phillips, Herbert P. 18, 29n
Piore, M.J. 31, 56n
political economy 6, 21, 95-6
port facilities 38-41, 48-9
Porter, Michael E. 7, 12n, 71, 81n
potential 21-2
Poynter, T.A. 71, 81n
Prescott, Kate 21-2, 28n
prices 4-5, 8, 33, 62
privatisation 23
product cycles, shortening 71
production 6-8, 20, 25, 42-3, 45, 65
products 6-7, 19-20, 45, 71-2
profits 6, 22, 62-3, 86
  in joint ventures in Yugoslavia
    118-21, 125, 128
protection 19, 33, 34, 156
public sector 98

quality control 19, 42, 62

raw materials 26, 40
recession 33
religion 16-17, 31, 41-2, 52, 53
Remmers, H. Lee 67, 78n
research and development (R&D)
  6-8, 67, 69, 86, 97-8, 136,
  142, 156
resources 24, 38, 46-8, 76
  allocation 6, 21, 68-9, 73, 75
  in alliances between firms 90-1, 95
Ricardian Theory 20
Richardson, G.B. 73, 75-6, 81n, 90-1,
  99n
Robinson, John 87, 88n
Rokkan, Stein 18, 29n
Rugman, Alan M. 9, 12n, 19, 29n,
  61, 62, 68-9, 81n, 87, 88n
Rumelt, Richard P. 66, 81n
rural culture 31, 40, 43, 48, 52

Salancik, Gerald 9, 12n, 63, 81n
San Marino 107

Scandinavia 70
Scherer, F.M. 6, 12n
Schumpeter, Josef 9-10, 16, 29n,
  30, 36, 57n, 86, 89n
scientific outlook and systems
  thinking 41-2, 46, 51
service industries 14, 25-6, 72
Singapore 24, 55, 157-8
Single European Act 20, 97, 156
Sloan, Alfred P. 67
Smith, Adam 10, 12n, 16, 29n
Smith, D.H. 30, 56n
Sogo Shosha (Japanese general
  trading companies) 26, 73, 76-7
Sony 157-8
South America 153, 158-9
South Korea 10, 33, 157-8
Soviet Union 158
Spain 150
state, the 10, 23
Steer, Peter 76. 81n
Stopford, John 67, 81n
strategy-structure approach to
  organisation of MNEs 65-6
Streeten, P. 54, 56n
Sweden 106-7, 117, 133, 135
Switzerland 106-7, 117, 135
systems thinking 16, 41-2, 46, 51

Taiwan 55, 157-8
takeovers 72, 73, 94-5, 131, 153
tax 8, 40, 62, 76
technological
  alliances 90, 93-4
  elements in trade theory 18
  knowhow 42
  lead 7
technology 6, 8, 17, 19-20, 23, 26,
  33, 36, 97, 128
  information technology develop-
    ment projects in Japan 142-4
  transfer 24, 33, 50-1, 125-6
Teece, David J. 62, 64, 65, 86, 89n,
  95, 99n
Thailand 157-8
Thanheiser, Heinz T. 66, 79n
Thurwell, Jane 70, 79n
tourism 151

Toynbee, Arnold 17, 29n
Toyne, Brian 15, 29n
Toyota Motor Corp. 142
trading system, global
  geographical and cultural
    factors in 45-50, 54-6
transaction cost economics approach
  to the organisation of MNEs
  61-5, 73, 74-5, 86
transport costs 20, 65, 137
transportation 37-41, 46
  water 38-40, 46-50
trust 25, 35-6, 44-5, 75, 83
Turk, Jeremy 64, 75, 80n

United Nations Centre on Transnational Corporations (UNCTC)
  23, 25, 29n
United States of America 36, 66-7,
  70, 73, 76-7, 103-7, 114,
  117, 134, 149-51, 154-9
  activities in Japan 133-6, 140-2,
    145, 152-3
  car firms 20-1
  Japanese takeovers in 131, 153
urban culture 31, 40, 52
US-Canada Free Trade Agreement 20

Vahlne, Jan Erik 80n
Vernon, Raymond 87n, 89n
vertical integration 6, 8, 19, 62, 65,
  71, 86
village communities 40, 44
violence 52-3

wages 33, 52-3
Wallerstein, I. 31, 57n
Walters, P.G.P. 80n
Weber, Max 16, 29n
Welch, Laurence 81n
welfare 19, 23, 55, 83
  implications of MNEs and 6, 18,
    20-1, 83, 86, 88
Wells, Louis T. 67, 81n
West Germany 66, 76, 94, 106-7, 112,
  117, 129, 133, 135, 150, 155
White, R.G. 71, 81n
Wiener, M.J. 46, 57n
Wilkins, Mira 66, 81n
Williamson, Oliver 62, 64, 65, 67, 75,
  81n, 82n
Willman, Paul 64, 75, 80n
Winter, D.G. 57n
Witt, Stephen F. 151, 160n
Wolf, Bernard M. 6, 12n
women
  employment in LDCs 23, 52-3
World Bank 157
Wrigley, Leonard 66, 82n

Yannopoulos, George N. 77, 82n
Yasuki, Hirohiko 76, 79n
Young, Stephen 71, 82n
Yugoslavia, joint ventures in 103-10
  legal regulations 110-13, 122
  motivation for 126-9
  route to 122-6
  success of 118-22
  survey of firms in 113-18